A Visitor's Guide

The Battle of Cambrai 1917

Mœuvres and Bourlon, Cantaing and Graincourt to Flesquières, Masnières, Gouzeaucourt and Gonnelieu

Tank H.1 Hilda *of H Battalion on a railway truck at the Fins railhead, 6 December 1917. Hilda was the tank in which Brigadier General Hugh Elles led the tanks into action on 20 November. The tank, commanded by Second Lieutenant Thomas Leach, was eventually ditched in front of Ribécourt.*

A Visitor's Guide

The Battle of Cambrai 1917

Mœuvres and Bourlon, Cantaing and Graincourt to Flesquières, Masnières, Gouzeaucourt and Gonnelieu

Jerry Murland

Pen & Sword
MILITARY

CONTENTS

Introduction and Acknowledgements ix
Visiting Military Cemeteries 1
Historical Context 4
Visiting the Area 15

Route 1:   Havrincourt 19
Route 2:   Ribécourt-la-Tour and Flesquières 28
Route 3:   Mœuvres 45
Route 4:   Graincourt-lès-Havrincourt 55
Route 5:   Cantaing-sur-Escaut and Fontaine-Notre-Dame 61
Route 6:   Bourlon 76
Route 7:   Marcoing and Masnières 93
Route 8:   Villers-Plouich and La Vacquerie 118
Route 9:   Gouzeaucourt and Gonnelieu 129
Route 10:   Car Tour 146

Appendix 1: VC Winners during the Cambrai Offensive 169
Appendix 2: Writers, Artists, Poets and Composers who Took
             Part in the Cambrai Offensive 172
Further Reading 174
Index 176

INTRODUCTION AND ACKNOWLEDGEMENTS

The *Visitor's Guide to The Battle of Cambrai 1917* is the ninth in a series of guidebooks in which routes have been designed to provide the battlefield tourist with the opportunity of appreciating and exploring the more remote parts of the battlefield. The guide does not intend to be a definite account of the battle but merely an opportunity to explore an area of the Western Front which, until now, has been neglected when compared with the Somme and Arras. The Battle of Cambrai, also known as the First Battle of Cambrai, began in the utmost secrecy on the morning of 20 November 1917 and lasted until 7 December 1917. This guide is an attempt to look in detail at some of the locations that were fought over as the British front advanced towards Cambrai. The battlefield remains much as it was over 100 years ago and 9 locations have been chosen for more in-depth examination. Routes have been designed for the walker and cyclist and those locations not covered, such as **Noyelles** and **Trescault**, are visited in the car tour, which explores the whole battlefield. A SatNav with European maps is of obvious worth in your travels around the area and please make use of *Google Earth* or the French equivalent *Géoportail* before your visit to familiarize yourself with the area and the routes you intend to use.

Whilst I have ensured that vehicles are not left in isolated spots, it is highly recommended you take the usual precautions when leaving a vehicle unattended by placing valuables securely in the boot or out of sight and, being northern France, it is always advisable to carry a waterproof and wear a sensible pair of boots or shoes to walk in. Be aware that at the time of writing all routes have been thoroughly checked but occasionally gates and fences spring up without warning. Within the built-up areas cafes and refreshment stops are usually open during normal hours but it is a good idea to take something to eat and drink when away from your vehicle for any length of time. Cyclists will recognize the need to use multi-terrain tyres on their bikes and the benefits of a sturdier hybrid or off-road machine. Regular visitors to the battlefields will be familiar with the collections of old shells and other explosive material that is often placed at the roadside by farmers. By all means look and take photographs, but please do not touch as much of it is still in an unstable condition.

The historical information provided with each route has of necessity been limited but I have given an overview around which to develop your understanding of what took place and why. Nevertheless, there are some additional suggestions for further reading at the end of the book which should widen your appreciation of the events that took place on this sector. Appendix 1 contains a list of the Victoria Crosses that were awarded during the offensive and Appendix 2 gives details of some of the writers, artists, poets and composers that took part in the battle.

In acknowledging the assistance of others, I must thank **Paul Reed** for his generosity in lending me his copy of *Following the Tanks* and **Philippe Gorczynski** for his help with some of the routes. **Steve Binks** very kindly trusted me with his collection of trench maps of the Cambrai area for which I am very grateful and **Jack Sheldon** has been of great help. He finally solved the question of Talma Chateau in Marcoing and has also allowed me to quote from his excellent book *The German Army at Cambrai*. My eternal thanks must go to **Jérémy Bourdon** who made up for my camera theft by taking the photographs that were contained therein and thus contributed to the presentation of the guide, many thanks for your help Jérémy. The guide would have been much less colourful without the inclusion of quotations and, wherever possible, all reasonable attempts have been made to trace and contact copyright owners; where this has not been successful, please contact the publisher so that any omissions or errors may be corrected. I should also add that any mistakes in the text are mine alone. Last, but by no means least, I must thank my wife Joan who has yet again tolerated my absence from family life and supported me throughout this project.

VISITING MILITARY CEMETERIES

The concept of the **Imperial War Graves Commission (IWGC)** was created by **Fabian Ware** (1869–1949), the volunteer leader of a Red Cross mobile unit which saw service on the Western Front for most of the period of the war. Concern for the identification and burial of the dead led Ware to begin lobbying for an organization devoted to burial and maintenance of those who had been killed or died in the service of their country. On 21 May 1917 the Prince of Wales became the president of the IWGC with **Fabian Ware** as its vice-chairman. Forty-three years later the IWGC became the **Commonwealth War Graves Commission (CWGC)**. Neither a soldier nor a politician, Ware was later honoured with a knighthood and held the honorary rank of major general. He died in 1949. The commission was responsible for introducing the standardized headstone which would bring equality in death regardless of rank, race or creed and it is this familiar headstone that you will see now in CWGC cemeteries all over the world.

Major General Fabian Ware (left) with King George V (far right) at Tyne Cot Cemetery in 1922. Standing behind the king is Field Marshall Sir Douglas Haig.

CWGC cemeteries are usually well signposted with the familiar green and white direction indicators and where there is a CWGC plot within a communal cemetery, such as **Bourlon Communal Cemetery**, the green and white sign at the entrance, with the words *Tombes de Guerre du Commonwealth*, indicates their presence. The tall Cross of Sacrifice with the bronze Crusader's sword can be found in many cemeteries where

The green and white CWGC signpost marks the way to military cemeteries throughout the French and Belgian battlefields.

there are relatively large numbers of dead. The larger cemeteries also have the rectangular shaped Stone of Remembrance. A visitor's book and register of casualties is usually kept in a bronze box by the entrance. CWGC cemeteries are noted for their high standards  of horticultural excellence and the image of rows of headstones set amidst grass pathways and flowering shrubs is one every battlefield visitor takes away with them. On each headstone is the badge of the regiment or corps or, in the case of Commonwealth forces, the national emblem. Below that is the name and rank of the individual and the date on which they died together with any decoration they may have received. Where the headstone marks the grave of a non-Christian, the emblem most commonly associated with their faith replaces the simple cross. Headstones of Victoria Cross winners, such as **Brigadier General Roland Bradford**, have the additional motif of the decoration inscribed on it. At the base of the headstone is often an inscription chosen by the family. Headstones marking the unidentified bear the inscriptions chosen by Rudyard Kipling, 'A Soldier of the Great War' or 'Known unto God'. Special memorials are erected to casualties known to be buried in the cemetery but whose precise location is uncertain. It is inevitable that the visitor will come across cemeteries that contain men who were killed in 1918 during the Second Battle of Cambrai, some cemeteries such as **Cantaing British Cemetery** and **Masnières British Cemetery** contain only men who were killed in 1918, others have a mixture of men killed in both campaigns. The 1918 cemeteries have not been fully described unless there is a grave of some note.

Brigadier General Roland Bradford's headstone in Hermies British Cemetery is of a standard pattern which you will find across all Second and First World War CWGC cemeteries. Post-war CWGC headstones have a notch cut into either shoulder at the top.

German Cemeteries

The German War Graves Commission – **Volksbund Deutsche Kriegsgräberfürsorge** – is responsible for the maintenance and upkeep of German war graves in Europe and North Africa. Apart from some scattered German headstones in CWGC cemeteries, the main German cemetery, where almost 10,000 casualties are buried or remembered in the ossuary, is **Cambrai East Military Cemetery** on Rue de Solesmes in Cambrai.

Equivalent Ranks

I have produced a rough guide to German, French and British equivalent ranks which should assist you when visiting the cemeteries and memorials referred to in the guidebook and understanding the ranks of those mentioned in the text.

British	German	French
Field Marshall	*Generalfeldmarschall*	*Maréchal de France*
General	*Generaloberst*	*Général d'Armée*
Lieutenant General	*General der Infantrie/Artillerie Kavallerie*	*Général de Corps Armée*
Major General	*Generalmajor*	*Général de Division*
Brigadier General	No equivalent rank	*Général de Brigade*
Colonel	*Oberst*	Colonel
Lieutenant Colonel	*Oberstleutnant*	Lieutenant Colonel
Major	*Major*	*Commandant/Major*
Captain	*Hauptmann/Rittmeister*	*Capitaine*
Lieutenant	*Oberleutnant*	Lieutenant
Second Lieutenant	*Leutnant*	*Sous Lieutenant*
Warrant Officer	*Feldwebelleutnant*	*Adjutant*
Sergeant Major	*Offizierstellvertreter*	*Sergent Major*
Sergeant	*Vizefeldwebel*	*Sergent*
Corporal	*Unteroffizer/Oberjäger*	*Caporal*
Lance Corporal	*Gefreiter/Obergefreiter*	No equivalent rank
Private Trooper Sapper	*Schütze/Grenadier/Jäger/ Musketier Soldat/Pionier/Fahrer/Füsilier Kanonier*	*Soldat, Chasseur Artilleur Légionnaire*

HISTORICAL CONTEXT

Proposals for a military operation in the Cambrai area using a large number of tanks originated with 37-year-old **Brigadier General Hugh Elles** and **Lieutenant Colonel John 'Boney' Fuller** of the Tank Corps during August 1917. Eventually a controversial plan for a limited attack or raid using a large number of tanks was accepted and **General Sir Julian Byng**, commander of the Third Army, convinced GHQ to use his sector of the line which included the unspoilt Artois fields west of Cambrai that were considered to be ideal for tanks. In 1917, Churchill, in his capacity as Minister of Munitions, advocated the enemy on the Western Front would only be defeated by mechanical means and not by manpower alone and such mechanical means should be accompanied by the element of surprise. He was evidently keen on the use of tanks but up until November 1917 the tank had a difficult career as a military weapon of war. Indeed, it was on the mind of every officer and man of the Tank Corps that Cambrai was perhaps the last throw of the dice for the much-maligned tank as a viable battlefield weapon. The opportunity presented itself early on the morning of 20 November when the Tank Corps came of age, yet it was not until the BEFs all-arms attacks in the latter half of 1918 that they finally took their rightful place on the battlefield. The Battle of Cambrai 1917 was later considered a turning point in the

General Sir Julian Byng.

Brigadier General Hugh Elles.

Lieutenant Colonel John Fuller.

Freepost Plus RTKE-RGRJ-KTTX
Pen & Sword Books Ltd
47 Church Street
BARNSLEY
S70 2AS

DISCOVER MORE ABOUT PEN & SWORD BOOKS

Pen & Sword Books have over 4000 books currently available, our imprints include; Aviation, Naval, Military, Archaeology, Transport, Frontline, Seaforth and the Battleground series, and we cover all periods of history on land, sea and air.

Can we stay in touch? From time to time we'd like to send you our latest catalogues, promotions and special offers by post. If you would prefer not to receive these, please tick this box. ☐

We also think you'd enjoy some of the latest products and offers by post from our trusted partners: companies operating in the clothing, collectables, food & wine, gardening, gadgets & entertainment, health & beauty, household goods, and home interiors categories. If you would like to receive these by post, please tick this box. ☐

We respect your privacy. We use personal information you provide us with to send you information about our products, maintain records and for marketing purposes. For more information explaining how we use your information please see our privacy policy at www.pen-and-sword.co.uk/privacy. You can opt out of our mailing list at any time via our website or by calling 01226 734222.

Mr/Mrs/Ms ....

Address...

Postcode.......................... Email address...............................

Website: www.pen-and-sword.co.uk Email: enquiries@pen-and-sword.co.uk
Telephone: 01226 734555   Fax: 01226 734438
Stay in touch: facebook.com/penandswordbooks or follow us on Twitter @penswordbooks

war and Byng was honoured by having his temporary rank of general made substantive.

Conscious of needing a victory and very much aware that the Prime Minister, David Lloyd George, was critical of his every move, particularly after the pitiful tragedy of Third Ypres, Sir Douglas Haig decided in his wisdom to change the mode of attack into a full-blown minor offensive. The Cambrai offensive was thus limited by the forces available and a timescale of 48 hours, the lack of forces exacerbated to a great extent by the Italian disaster at Caporetto in October 1917 which resulted in Haig being instructed to send two divisions to Italy post-haste under the command of General Herbert Plumer. If ever a Commander-in-Chief needed some sort of victory, it was now.

For the assault on Cambrai, Byng was allocated 7 infantry divisions plus 2 in reserve, 5 cavalry divisions and 3 tank brigades. The Hindenburg Line was to be breached on a 6-mile front between the Canal du Nord (under construction and effectively a dry ditch) on the left and the Canal de Saint-Quentin on the right. The Infantry, organized into IV Corps under **Lieutenant General Sir William Pultney**, III Corps under **Lieutenant General Sir Charles Woollcombe** and VII Corps under **Lieutenant General Sir Thomas Snow**, would, together with the tanks, capture the dominating Flesquières and Bourlon Ridges. The Cavalry Corps, exploiting the gap opened up by the capture of Fontaine-Notre-Dame, would advance on Cambrai, an important rail junction, which would by its capture cause the Germans considerable logistic problems. The break in the Hindenburg Line would expose the German Army in the area to the risk of having their line rolled up to the north

Lieutenant General Sir William Pultney.

Lieutenant General Sir Charles Woollcombe.

Lieutenant General Sir Thomas Snow.

and, if the penetration was deep enough, a breakthrough could threaten the whole German defensive system. Thus, the original plan had progressed from a tank raid of some 48 hours' duration to an optimistic offensive designed to capture and consolidate ground, circumstances that are not unfamiliar to students of the First World War.

The Hindenburg Line

In order to shorten the line and release some divisions after the Battle of the Somme in 1916 Field Marshal von Hindenburg ordered the construction of a new line to which the German Army withdrew in March 1917. The line was one of the most impressive ground fortifications ever constructed in Europe, five sections each named after a German hero comprising a massive system that ran from Arras in the north to Laffaux, near Soissons on the Aisne, in the south. Each system was protected by at least five belts of wire some 50ft deep and 3ft high and aerial photographs showed them to be laid out geometrically, funnelling any attacking force into killing zones. In the Cambrai sector the first line facing the British was the *Siegfriedstellung* (Hindenburg Line) running in a general northwesterly direction for a distance of 6 miles from the Canal de Saint-Quentin at Bantex to Havrincourt. At Havrincourt the line turned north along the line of the Canal du Nord to reach Mœuvres. At varying distances behind the first line lay the second and third main German defences known as the *Siegfried Zwischenstellung* (Hindenburg Support Line) and the *Siefried II Zwischenstellung* (Marcoing–Beaurevoir–Masnières Line).

A tank crushing the wire on the Hindenburg Line.

The trenches themselves were up to 12ft wide at the top creating a difficulty for the British Mark IV tank which was only 10ft long. During the retreat to the Hindenburg Line, the area over which the Germans were withdrawing was methodically and cold-bloodedly destroyed to delay troops from following too closely. Villages were torn down, water sources poisoned, trees cut down, roads blown up and delayed-action fuses planted in major buildings; the rolling countryside was reduced to a wilderness and the scars of war turned the landscape into a desolate and pathetic sight. News of the demolitions as well as the deplorable condition of French civilians left by the Germans were serious blows to German prestige in neutral countries.

The Role of the Artillery
Masterminded by **Brigadier General Henry Tudor**, one of the pioneers of scientific artillery work, there were a number of innovative features associated with the British plan for the assault on Cambrai. The first, and probably the most remarkable, was the attack largely kept as a complete surprise to the Germans. Known as Operation GY to preserve secrecy, this meant that elaborate precautions were taken prior to the attack to conceal the build-up of men and materiel and in particular there was no preliminary artillery bombardment. This unusual step flew in the face of previous attacks where the gunners had registered their guns on targets with ranging shots prior to the assault, thereby warning the Germans that an attack was imminent. Instead, predicted fire or 'shooting off the map' was the order of the day. Another feature of the opening artillery barrage was the pauses on each of the German defence lines. This was a lifting or jumping barrage, as opposed to a creeping barrage, for example, in the IV Corps sector the barrage lifted nine times between the first German line and the Flesquières Ridge. The success of such a plan relied almost entirely on 3 Field Survey Company whose tasks it was to carry out observation techniques such as flash spotting and sound ranging using listening stations. To put it simply, each round of artillery fire produced a sound wave and by measuring the distance the point from which the sound wave came from could be determined precisely. In all at least 1,003 guns, over half of which were 18-pounder field guns, were in action on 20 November on a front extending some 6 miles. **Major Edward Norton**, commanding D Battery RHA, commented that the batteries on **Hubert Road** in Havrincourt Wood were literally flank to flank in two long lines as far as the eye could see.

A new fuse, which had first been used during the Third Battle of Ypres, was to be employed extensively at Cambrai. The fuse 106 was able to detonate the shell on impact with the wire or ground, the blast travelling outwards rather than upwards, which considerably reduced the initial barrage on 20 November and avoided churning up the ground in the form of craters, making it difficult for the infantry to advance and almost impossible for tanks to proceed. What is perhaps not fully appreciated is that where the gunners could not follow the tanks some 700 fascines were also issued to batteries to fill in trenches in order to get the guns across the wide trenches.

Private Billy Kirby of the 2/6 West Yorkshires, who was waiting south of Havrincourt with his battalion, was one of the men who were stunned by the sheer ferocity of the bombardment as it opened up on the German lines:

> Though the ground shook with the thunder of the massed guns, it was the breathtaking circle of multi-coloured flame rising like millions of gigantic fireworks, which produced a sight so breathtaking, so altogether awe-inspiring, as to root us to the ground, unable to take our eyes away from the beauty of man's explosive power appearing like some ethereal glory rather than the concentrated hellish force which would tear men apart, leaving them little more than shapeless, shattered flesh and blood.

The Tank Corps

At Cambrai, 476 Tanks, of which 378 were Mark IV fighting tanks, were used in what was described as the first battle where tanks had the principal task. The Mark IV, developed from the Mark I and II, went into production in March 1917 and was powered by

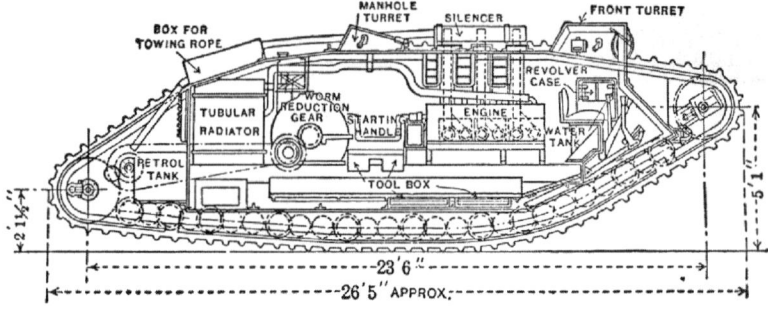

The Mark IV tank.

a 195hp Daimler engine with a maximum speed of 3.7mph over good ground. The male tank was armed with machine guns and two Hotchkiss 6-pounders, which were mounted in two sponsons on either side, whilst the female was equipped only with machine guns. The crew was made up of an officer and seven other ranks but could increase to nine if the section commander decided to come on board. A section of three or four tanks was commanded by a captain whilst a company of four sections was the preserve of a major. Three companies made up a battalion under the command of a lieutenant colonel. Each of the nine battalions of tanks at Cambrai had its own number and in many cases this was supplemented with the name of the tank painted on both sides and the front of the tank. As for the period preceding the assault, D, E and G Battalions were in Havrincourt Wood, A, H and B Battalions were in Dessart Wood, C Battalion was at Villers-Guislain and I and F Battalions were in Gouzeaucourt Wood.

In addition to the 378 fighting tanks, others were designated for specific tasks. The thirty-two wire-pulling tanks were tasked with creating a gap in the wire to clear the way for the infantry and cavalry. The grapnel hooks attached to each tank tore the wire from their supports, although one man occasionally had to exit the tank in order to attach the grapnel in the appropriate place. The special

Mark IV tanks equipped with fascines prior to unloading at the Fins railhead.

supply tanks were used to pull three sledges delivering 14 tons of petrol, oil, grease and ammunition. These tanks with unarmed sponsons were some of the older Mark I, II and III models salvaged from the Somme and Arras. The remainder consisted of wireless tanks, cavalry bridging tanks and a gun-carrier tank with 4 tons of supplies. At Cambrai there were several other pieces of equipment designed to ease the passage of tanks across trenches and uneven ground. The first of these was the fascine, which was in effect formed from huge bundles of branches held together by two chains. A fascine was 10ft long and weighed 1.75 tons and was held above the tank with a release mechanism in the cabin which allowed the bundle to be dropped.

Although the ditching beam had been in use before the Cambrai offensive, this large wooden beam, reinforced with sheet metal, lay across the corner posts of the two top rails on the tank. When the tank was stuck, the beam, attached by two chains to the tracks, was dropped, giving the tank a chance to free itself by getting a grip on the beam.

Nevertheless, despite the improvements and developments, serving in a Mark IV tank was incredibly noisy to the extent that conversation was impossible. Temperatures of about 45 degrees centigrade were commonplace inside a cabin that was shrouded in darkness, light only coming in through the slits in the outer armour. After just a few minutes as the tank got up to speed the cabin was filled with the smell of burning oil and petrol which, together with the exhaust fumes and steam from the cooling system, contributed to the crew suffering nausea and vomiting. During the battle a hit by machine guns on the outside wall of the tank produced splinters from the inside armour plating which could cause flesh wounds that quickly became infected, and it was said that after several hours inside a tank the crew needed at least 1 to 2 hours to recover. That was all well and good, but during the Cambrai offensive 22-year-old **Captain Daniel Hickey**, the author of *Rolling into Action*, when parking his tanks at Orival Wood after his men had liberated Fontaine-Notre-Dame, remarked that his crews had been fighting for at least 11 hours

Captain Daniel Hickey of H Battalion.

continuously. Although a number of tanks failed to start or were ditched, the greatest losses were caused by fire and crews, providing they survived, were often unable to exit the tank in the case of a direct hit from German artillery. Being in the Tank Corps in the First World War was a debilitating and hazardous business. **Major Douglas Wimberley**, of the 51st Division Machine Gun Corps, came across a horrific sight outside Cantaing:

> A half burnt tank straddled half across the road and outside the door were two dead members of the crew, blackened and half burnt, one had an appalling wound in the body as he tried to get out at the door, and his entrails were out of his body in the road. It nearly made me sick.

Wimberley goes on to say that for days afterwards horses shied violently at the place, smelling the blood and burnt flesh. It is worth remembering that of the 242 tank crew killed at Cambrai, over 163 individuals have no known graves.

The Attack

The attack began with high hopes, sustained by the excellent initial progress on 20 and 21 November. It is interesting to note that the line of attack of all the British divisions is skewed from right to left from the line of the roads rather than following the direction of the roads themselves. The actual target of the assault was not the town of Cambrai itself but the commanding heights of the ridge capped by **Bourlon Wood**, from where Cambrai and the ground beyond lay at the mercy of the British. Described as the first battle in history to be founded on the internal combustion engine, the first day of the assault began at 6.20am with a short barrage of high explosive and smoke to cover the first advances. By the end of the first day the German positions had been breached to a depth of 3 to 4 miles, over 4,000 prisoners and 100 guns had been captured and British casualties were little more than 4,000. On the III Corps front the Hindenburg Line was breached and the crossings over the canal at **Masnières** and **Marcoing** had been completed. Of the two assault divisions of IV Corps, the 62nd Division made good progress aided by the 36th Division. **Havrincourt**, **Graincourt** and **Anneux** were captured and by dusk on the first day 186 Brigade had reached the main road running from Bapaume to Cambrai. However, at **Flesquières** the 51st (Highland) Division was stopped after the majority of tanks assigned to the attack were put out of action, but

H.45 Hyacinth *(H Battalion) was initially ditched in a German trench near Ribécourt whilst supporting men of the 1/Leicestershire.*

it was enough to prompt the bells in England to ring out in triumph at the 'breakthrough'. Nevertheless, at the end of the first day the Tank Corps had lost 179 tanks from a combination of mechanical breakdowns, ditching and direct hits from enemy artillery and the gap between Marcoing and Masnières had not been opened up for the cavalry to advance through. Poor communication and leadership of the main cavalry force was intensified by the fact that overall command of the cavalry was too far in the rear, which in reality meant the huge hole on the German line remained unexploited.

Flesquières along with **Cantaing** was taken the next day but **Bourlon Wood** became the scene of a bloody conflict, reminiscent of High Wood on the Somme a year earlier. Haig had hoped to be on top of the high ground at Bourlon by this time, but British forces were making little discernible progress. He had initially limited the offensive to 48 hours and that time was now up. Faced with a hard choice, withdraw from Bourlon or press ahead with the offensive, he chose the latter just as the British advance was beginning to crumble in the face of German reserves.

As with the initial British advance, the German counterattack of 30 November was completely unexpected and spelled the end of any thoughts Haig may have had regarding reaching Cambrai. German infantry attacked in small groups, bypassing the centres of resistance and employing a modus operandi that had been developed in Russia and would be seen again during the German advance of 21 March 1918. The German attack in the north was considerably less effective than that of the south around Villers-Guislain and after grimly hanging on for a week, the British fell back to the 'Winter Line' on 6 December, leaving a salient around Flesquières and conceding **Gonnelieu** and **Villers-Guislain**. Today, Cambrai is largely remembered as an indicator of future warfare and, in heralding the German tactics of 1940, brought the war firmly into the twentieth century. Nevertheless, despite the British success of the first day, the offensive fell considerably short of what had been envisaged. Mistakes were mainly due to an inability to understand and exploit a fight in open country, the German counterattack suffering from the same faults, the momentum and drive were not sustained due to an inflexibility in fighting in open country. Nevertheless, Cambrai 1917 was one of the most evenly balanced battles in history.

Air Support
Although many accounts rarely mention the fact, a considerable number of aircraft were assembled comprising twenty-six Royal Flying Corps (RFC) and Royal Naval Air Service (RNAS) squadrons. Over 290 Sopwith Camels and Scouts, Bristol Fighters and DH.4s and 5s from III Brigade, including a section of 49 Squadron for daylight bombing, together with the aircraft of 1 Brigade equipped with Camels, SE.5s and DH.4s, were tasked with bombing the railway stations at Somain and Dechy and carrying out offensive patrols between Douai and the Sensée Valley. In the two days before the attack, aircraft noise had been used to mask the tanks as they moved up for the attack. Despite the battlefield being shrouded in thick, patchy fog, the aircraft engaged enemy troops with machine guns and small bombs. Whilst pursuing their ground-attack role, many pilots dropped down to only 30ft to press their attacks, braving ferocious volumes of ground fire directed at them. They were highly effective, at times even saving the tanks from being pinned down. But the cost to the airmen was high. Meanwhile, the German ground-attack patrols *(Schlachtstaffeln)* used the all-metal armoured Junkers J1 and the Halberstadt CL.II effectively which had a significant debilitating effect on British troops, both physically and in terms of morale. In addition, the German infantry quickly learned how to fight back against low-flying aircraft, and once air reinforcements

The German Halberstadt CL.II.

arrived the loss rate of ground-attack aircraft was as high as 30 per cent of aircraft deployed. For example, 3 Squadron, flying Sopwith Camels, lost eight aircraft on 20 November in a disastrous attack on Estourmel, Carnières and Caudry, although exactly which machines were lost where is still uncertain. Two more aircraft were lost over Bourlon Wood on 23 November and a further three on 30 December.

VISITING THE AREA

Visitors to the area can stay either in Cambrai or take advantage of the profusion of bed-and-breakfast and self-catering establishments in the area. I can recommend the three-star **Hotel Beatus** on the Avenue de Paris, Cambrai. The hotel is excellent and has the added advantage of being owned by Phillipe Gorczynski. I can also personally recommend the centrally based **Clos Saint-Jacques** guesthouse on Rue St-Jacques, Cambrai, which offers bed and breakfast and has four high-quality rooms. Another good bed-and-breakfast hotel is **Le 1880** on Avenue de Valenciennes, which again is centrally located and boasts a shared lounge and kitchen with dishwasher. All three of these establishments are handy for visits to the **German Cemetery** and the **Porte de Paris Communal Cemetery**. Campers will find the Municipal Campsite at **Les 3 Clochers** on Rue Jean Goude at Cambrai to be of reasonable quality but may have to look to the north of the city to find a site on which to base a holiday of more than a few days.

The three-star Hotel Beatus is in the Avenue de Paris, Cambrai.

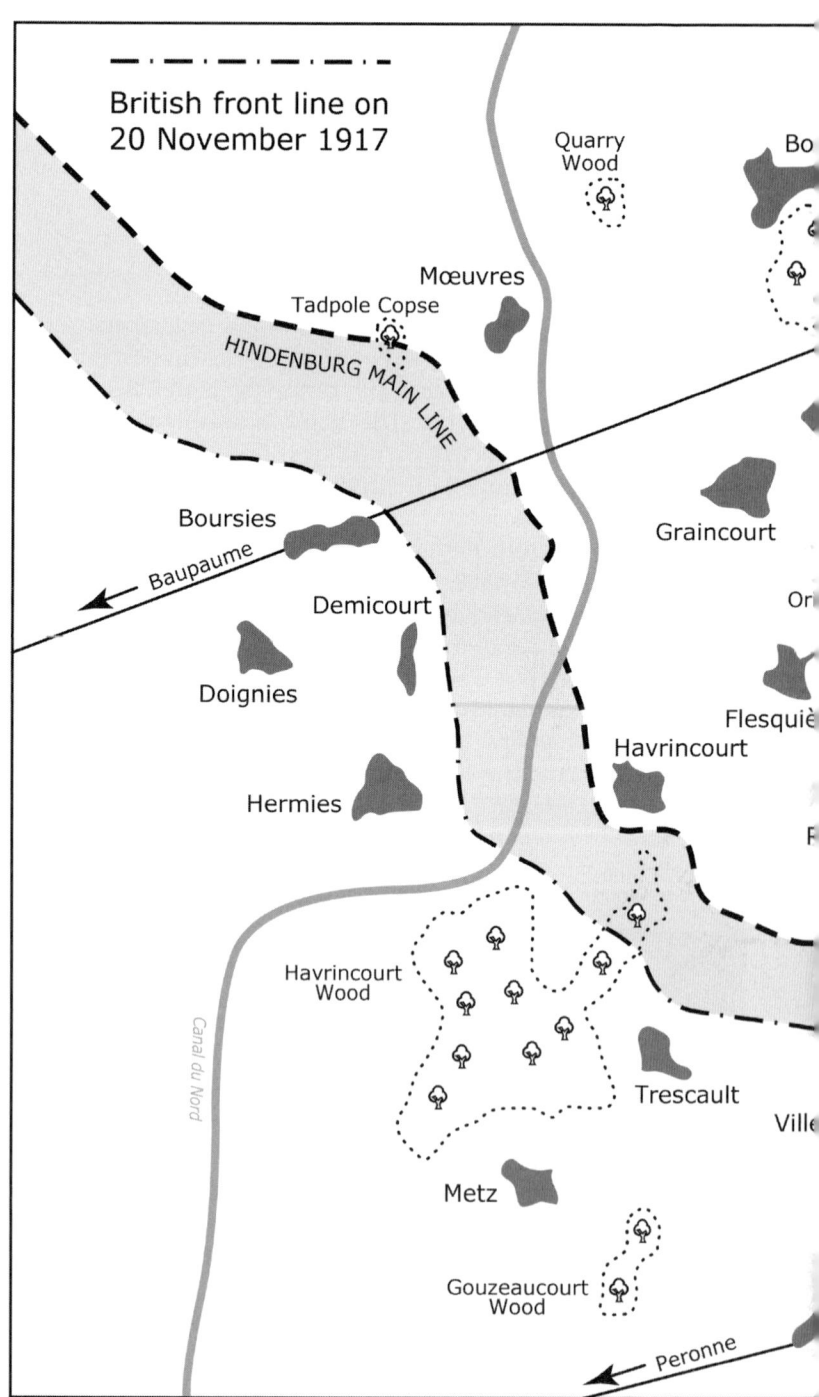

A simplified map showing the principal towns and villages involved in the conflict.

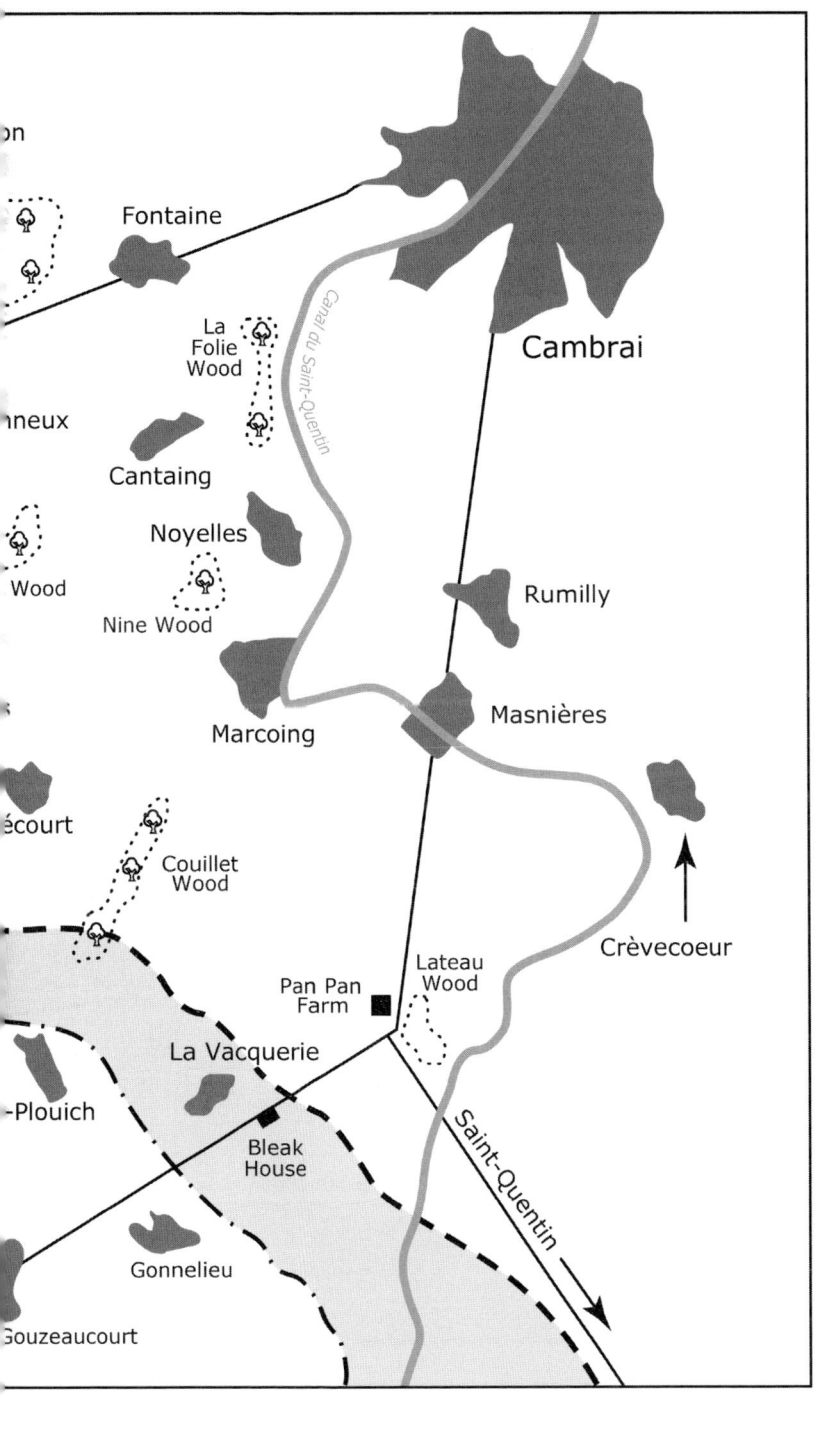

Abbreviations

In compiling the guide I have taken the liberty of using a number of abbreviations in the text. With some German units I have simply trimmed Infantry Regiment and Reserve Infantry Regiment to IR and RIR. Thus, Infantry Regiment No. 84 becomes IR84, Reserve Infantry Regiment No. 165 becomes RIR165 and Fusilier Infantry Regiment 40 becomes FIR40. Similarly, Grenadier Infantry Regiment becomes GIR whilst Field Artillery Regiment has been abbreviated to FAR. German divisions have been abbreviated to ID, likewise Bavarian Infantry Division becomes BID. British battalions and units have also been abbreviated after their first mention in the text, for example, the 1/Royal Guernsey Light Infantry becomes 1/RGLI.

Summary of Routes

To assist you in your choice of route I have provided a summary of all ten routes in the guidebook together with an indication as to their suitability for walkers, cyclists or car tourists. Approximate distances are in km – the first figure in the table – and miles, whilst the circular alpha/numeric references in the text of each route correspond directly with those on the relevant map. I hope you enjoy exploring the Cambrai battlefields as much as I have done.

Route Number	Route	Distance	🚶	🚲	🚗
1	Havrincourt	6.4km/4.2 miles	✓	✓	
2	Ribécourt-la-Tour and Flesquières	6.5km/4.3 miles	✓	✓	
3	Mœuvres	10.2km/6.3 miles	✓	✓	
4	Graincourt-lès Havrincourt	2.3km/1.4 miles	✓	✓	✓
5	Cantaing-sur-Escaut and Fontaine-Notre-Dame	8.1km/5.7 miles	✓	✓	
6	Bourlon	7.5km/4.6 miles	✓	✓	
7	Marcoing and Masnières	4.7km/2.9 miles	✓	✓	✓
8	Villers-Plouich and La Vacquerie	3.8km/2.3 miles	✓	✓	
9	Gouzeaucourt and Gonnelieu	7.1km/4.4miles	✓	✓	
10	Car Tour	56km/35 miles		✓	✓

Route 1

Havrincourt

A circular tour beginning at: the former railway station

Distance: 6.9km/4.29 miles
Grade: Easy
Suitable for: 🚶 🚴
Map: Cambrai-Bertincourt 2507 SB

General description and context: Havrincourt was captured by the 62nd Division on 20 November but lost in March 1918. It was recaptured again by the 62nd Division in September 1918. The route begins at the railway station building and heads south along the D15 turning along the D5 and visiting the site of **Vesuvius** before continuing across the motorway to the canal bridge. Retracing the route to Vesuvius, we visit the site of **Etna** and the former **Dean Copse** before returning to the D15. On the way north we pass the sites of **Boggat Hole** and **Snowden** before returning to the roundabout north of Havrincourt Chateau. A right turn will take you past the site of Second Lieutenant McElroy's DSO action and the granite memorial to the 62nd (West Riding) Division before visiting **Grand Ravine British Cemetery**.

In November 1917 the Hindenburg Line (*Siegfriedstellung*) ran through the village south of the chateau and the present-day **Grand Ravine British Cemetery**. The British front line was to the south and Havrincourt Wood (Bois d'Havrincourt) was largely behind British lines. **Fermy Wood**, the northern part of Havrincourt Wood, had been reduced in size somewhat by the Germans as they withdrew to the Hindenburg Line in order to give their artillery and infantry improved fields of fire. The construction of the Canal du Nord had reached Havrincourt in 1914 and in the winter of 1916–17 its incomplete earthworks were incorporated into the defences of the Hindenburg Line. There are no really old buildings in the village as everything was destroyed, either by the building of the German defences or by the two battles of Cambrai. The chateau had been rebuilt by 1925 along with the Church of St-Géry and the railway

20 • The Battle of Cambrai 1917

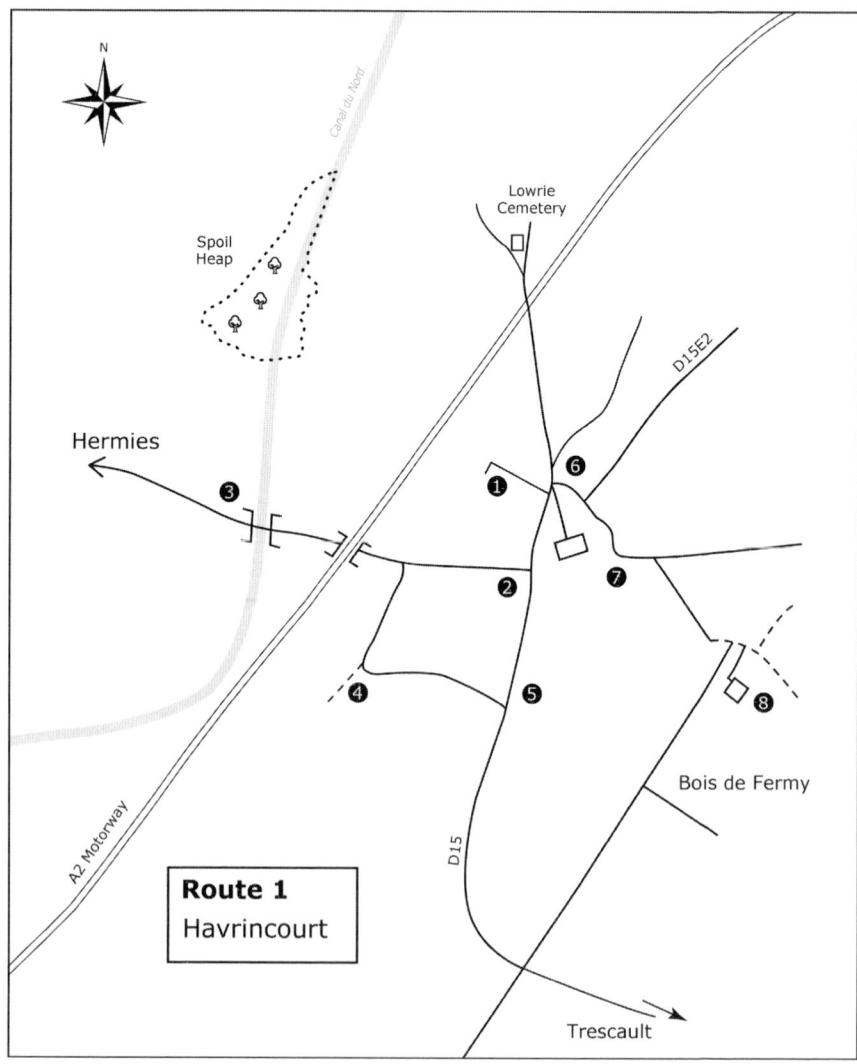

station. As for advance warning of the attack, it came during the early hours of 18 November when *Major* Fitz Hofmeister's IR84 raided a British outpost at **Trescault**, capturing a sergeant and five men of the 1/Royal Irish Fusiliers. Although they revealed a plan to attack Havrincourt, they were unable to give any more details, particularly about the huge troop concentrations in Havrincourt Wood. Two other raids were launched against the 55th and 20th Divisions and in the ensuing interrogations it was thought that an attack near Havrincourt was being prepared, possibly using a tank or two, although the date was largely unknown. It was enough though to put *Generalleutnant* Oskar von Watter and his Caudry Group on alert and the German Second Army moved one regiment and several artillery batteries to reinforce von Watter.

Prior to the attack, G Battalion of the Tank Corps was camouflaged in the bottom left-hand corner of Havincourt Wood, close to the D7 which runs from Ruyaulcourt to Metz-en-Couture, hereafter known as Metz, and D and E Battalions were in the bottom right-hand corner, where the wood crossed the D17 running from Metz to Trescault. On Hubert Road the guns stood almost wheel to wheel, **Major Ambrose Dudley** noting that 'artillery of all calibres: 18-pounders, heavy howitzers, and even super-heavy howitzers' were assembled and camouflaged with their limbers behind them. Then, at 1.00pm, much to the horror of the waiting tanks and infantry, a salvo of heavy German shells burst on **Oxford Valley**, a sunken road bisecting Hubert Road and running from Havrincourt into the wood. **Brigadier General Austin Anderson**, commanding the 62nd Division artillery, confessed to being anxious about the German artillery barrage and wondered if the 'Boche had some internal surprise in store'. In reality, it was probably von Watter's uneasiness that prompted the artillery barrage which fortunately did little damage, except to the men of the 1/5 Gordon Highlanders (153 Brigade) who were attacking Flesquières with the tanks of D Battalion. Many of them were caught waiting on the start line and a number were killed or wounded.

A total of sixty tanks were allocated to the 62nd Division attack on Havrincourt involving the whole of G Battalion with sixteen more tanks from D and E Battalions. On the left, 19/Company, under the command of **Major Francis Fernie**, was to lead 187 Brigade and on the right, 20 and 21/Companies, under the command of **Major Ralph Broome**, were to lead 185 Brigade. G Battalion probably had the most difficult time having to cross the centre of the wood to get to Oxford Valley, with only fifty tanks eventually taking part in the battle with four suffering from mechanical problems, one arriving late, two being impaled on tree stumps and a further

Major Broome commanded 20 and 21 Companies of tanks and led 185 Infantry Brigade into battle.

two being hit close to the start line. At 6.20am the men of Major General Walter Braithwaite's 62nd Division began their attack with 187 Brigade on the left with its left-flank battalion, the 2/5 King's Own Yorkshire Light Infantry (KOYLI), sandwiched between the Canal du Nord and the track running north from **Dean Copse**. The right-hand flank battalion of 185 Brigade, which was advancing on the right, was the 2/7 West Yorkshires whose objective was **Triangle Wood**. At 9.00am 186 Brigade, under the command of **Brigadier General Roland Bradford**, along with six tanks from G Battalion, moved off from Hubert Road and Shropshire Spur. By this time the Brigade Machine Gun Company was in action at **Butlers Cross** in support of the main attack, the route of which lay around the bottom of Havrincourt village, through Fermy Wood. The right-hand flank battalion, the 2/5 Duke of Wellingtons, was advancing along Oxford Road, passing **Boggat Hole** and **Snowden** before going west of the village towards the Blue Line.

Directions to start: Havrincourt is best approached from the D930 and the D15 which runs south and is probably the most direct route. If you are approaching the village from the direction of Metzen-Couture, then it is probably best to continue through Trescault and take the D15 into Havrincourt. Once in the village head for the chateau gates and the roundabout and park in Rue de la Gare.

Route description: Proceed along Rue de la Gare to ❶ the junction and turn right, following the D15 down to Rue d'Hermies. Turn right ❷ and proceed for 500m along the D5 to reach the site of **Vesuvius**. The former site of the crater covered the whole of the junction and was garrisoned by machine-gunners, in the event it was taken with a pincer movement, without waiting for the tanks, by the 2/4 and 2/5 KOYLI (187 Brigade). From **Vesuvius** continue straight ahead, crossing the motorway to reach the bridge(s) over the Canal du Nord, stop here ❸. If you look to the north for about 1,000m you may be able to see the **Spoilbank** on the left, made from excavations from the canal, captured by the 10/Royal Inniskilling Fusiliers (109 Brigade) on 20 November. Retrace your steps to the **Vesuvius** junction and turn right for 350m towards the approximate site of **Etna**, another crater which was strongly held by the Germans. As you pass over the former crater consider for a moment the demoralized defenders being overwhelmed by Yorkshire men at the point of the bayonet led by **Captain Alfred Lynn** and **Second Lieutenant William James** of the 2/5 KOYLI.

Sixty tanks were allocated to the 62nd Division attack.

About 140m from **Etna**, on the right of the track is the former site of **Dean Copse** ❹, there is also a crossroads of tracks here. Turn left and continue to the junction with the D15, turning left towards Havrincourt ❺. To the right is Havrincourt Chateau Park, private property, which hides the site of **Boggat Hole**, about 100m from the junction, amongst the undergrowth. (According to contemporary maps Boggat Hole was on the western side of the park.) Further on – about 250m from Boggat Hole – is the former site of **Snowden**, another fortified mine crater which took up most of the road opposite a gated farm building. Both of these strongpoints were taken by the 2/5 KOYLI.

From Snowden proceed to the junction with the D5. On the right-hand side of the D15 road, which leads from Havrincourt to Trescault, just before it turns left there is a **bunker**. This is hard to spot in the undergrowth of a wooded area (Chateau Wood) a little off the road. There are large, iron doors on the bunker, which was believed to have been a machine-gun post. Continue to the roundabout and stop at the chateau gates ❻. The building was occupied by the Germans to site machine guns, using them to fire on the 2/6th West Yorkshires. **Lieutenant Colonel Thomas Best**, commanding officer of the 2/5 Duke of Wellingtons, was killed

The chateau at Havrincourt, which dominates the roundabout.

by shots fired from the chateau or the adjoining park along with **Lieutenant George Bodker**, command devolving initially to the adjutant, Captain Herbert Jackson. Best and Bodker are buried in Ruyaulcourt Military Cemetery. It would appear that D Company of the 2/5 Duke of Wellingtons, under the command of **Captain Tom Goodall**, then cleared the chateau releasing from captivity a number of British prisoners who had been captured. The chateau, occupied by the Germans in both world wars, was destroyed in 1917, rebuilt and then destroyed again in the Second World War and once again rebuilt, in a similar style. If you continue north along the D15 you will reach Lowrie Cemetery which is just beyond the A2 motorway.

Continue over the roundabout, bearing right along **Rue des Calettes**, stopping at the village green and the church opposite the D15E2. Here you will find the imposing war memorial. The chateau and village still represented considerable opposition as German infantry fired down on the advancing troops from rooftops and high windows. **Private Billy Kirby** of the 2/6 West Yorkshires was aware that they were losing too many men:

> We were ordered to circle our final goal while our tanks made a frontal attack. While we entered the village from the rear, almost without opposition, the tanks crushed the enemy into complete surrender as they made their successful attack. But for

Havrincourt • 25

Lowrie Cemetery is concealed by a fork in the road on the D15.

these wonderful new weapons of war, our losses, as we sought to capture Haverincourt [sic], could have been staggering. As it was we found the German defenders lined up in the centre of the village – a tank standing by – the prisoners ready to move off into captivity.

There is no evidence to support the notion that the tank seen by Billy Kirby was G.3 *Gladiator*, commanded by **Second Lieutenant William McElroy**, but the tank was certainly in the centre of the village at the time. McElroy's tank had fallen into a large, water filled crater near the village green when a German bullet ignited the reserve petrol tank starting a fire. The crew escaped intact, but McElroy remained in the tank, killing eight of the surrounding enemy with his revolver and putting out the fire. Rejoining the tank, the crew then took around 100 German infantry captive. McElroy was awarded the DSO for his exploits.

From the village green continue along the road and round the sharp left-hand bend to the **62nd Division Memorial** ❼ on the right-hand side of the road. Unveiled in June 1922 by General Sir Robert Whigham, it sits on the site of a former German dugout some 30ft below. Further along the road you will see a CWGC signpost pointing the way to **Grand Ravine British Cemetery**. Follow the signpost for

The war memorial on the village green where William McElroy captured about 100 German infantrymen.

700m to the cemetery, situated in a shallow valley to the right of **Fermy Wood** ❽.

The cemetery consists of three rows of headstones, Row B was made by the 62nd Division Burial Officer in December 1917, whilst Rows A and C were made in 1918. There are 139 casualties buried here, 11 of them unidentified 1918 burials. The cemetery is situated at the western edge of the **Grand Ravine**, the same 'ravine' that you will park next to in Ribécourt. Stand at the entrance and cast your mind back to 20 November and imagine some 150 tanks leaving Fermy Wood, leading the infantry and advancing towards Ribécourt. The tanks allocated to the 62nd

The memorial to the men of the 62nd (West Riding) Division.

Division would have come through where you are standing. The noise and the sight of thousands of men of 185 and 187 Brigades advancing towards them must have been a terrifying sight for the defenders of Havrincourt. Just to the left of the cemetery the men of 186 Brigade moved towards their objectives at 9.00am. Thirty-three men, killed during the Cambrai offensive, are buried here and of these, there are twenty-four men of the 62nd Division killed between 22 and 29 November 1917 and one lone member of the RFC. **Air Mechanic 2nd Class William Roberts** (B.37) was attached to 175 Headquarters, Royal Field Artillery and killed on 3 December. A 36-year-old radio operator with 59 Squadron, his task would have been to relay messages from the squadron's RE8s to the artillery. If you are looking for a headstone on which to place your cross of remembrance, then look no further than **Lance Corporal Herbert Howell** (B2) of the West Yorkshire Regiment who was killed on 20 November 1917. From the cemetery retrace your steps past the monument and the scene of McElroy's DSO-winning action to reach your vehicle in Rue de la Gare.

Lance Corporal Herbert Howell.

Route 2
Ribécourt-la-Tour and Flesquières

A circular tour beginning at: the bridge at Ribécourt-la-Tour on the D89

Distance: 6.5km/4.3 miles
Grade: Moderate with some uphill sections
Suitable for: 🚶 🚴
Map: Cambrai-Bertincourt 2507 SB

General description and context: The route looks in particular at the 71 Brigade attack and the tank attack on Flesquières. Ribécourt-la-Tour, henceforth referred to as Ribécourt, was captured on the first day of the campaign by 71 Brigade (6th Division) and defended by the 387 Landwehr Infantry Regiment, under the command of *Oberstleutnant* von Wangenheim. The attack on Ribécourt and the Blue Line was supported by six sections of tanks from H Battalion followed 20 minutes later by a further two sections, whilst four sections of tanks, again from H Battalion, made up the third wave. Prior to the attack the Commander of 22 Company (H Battalion), **Major Gerald Huntbach**, was a little taken aback when **Brigadier General Hugh Elles** announced he would be leading the Tank Corps into battle in H.1 *Hilda*, commanded by **Second Lieutenant Thomas Leach**. After the tanks had rolled into no-man's-land **Captain Daniel Hickey** later wrote that Brigadier Elles was 'leading the attack with his head and shoulders sticking out of the top of the tank with his home made pennant flying proudly above him'. He remained there until *Hilda* ditched near **Plough Support Trench**, north of Villers-Plouich, and was seen tramping back to Beauchamp, pennant in hand. At 6.20am the 9/Norfolks, forming part of the second wave, advanced on the village. D Company was on the right, B Company in the centre with A Company on the left and C Company in support. **Lieutenant Colonel Bernard Prior**, commanding the Norfolks, noted that everything was going according to plan:

Ribécourt-la-Tour and Flesquières

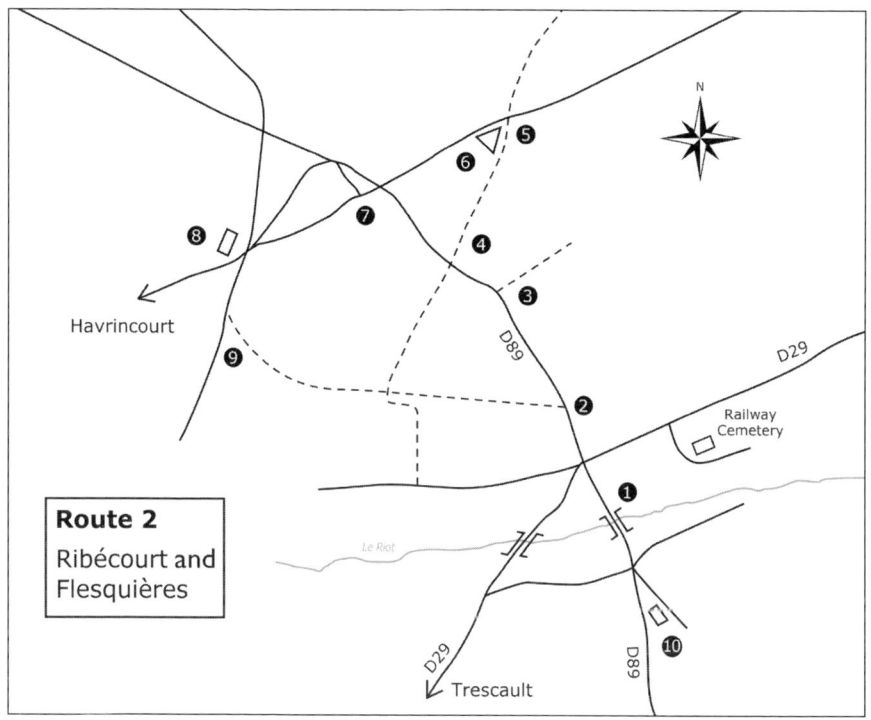

Route 2
Ribécourt and Flesquières

The leading tanks followed by the Leicesters were crossing trenches and were starting to cross No-Man's-Land, a wonderful sight in the half light. Ponderous, groaning, wobbling, these engines of war crawled, lurched their way towards the enemy's line, followed by groups of men in file. Overhead our shells were pouring over ... Neither tanks nor Leicesters were clear of our lines when we reached A Company. I have never seen men in better fighting spirit, they all stood up and cheered when I reached them.

Prior was north of Plush Trench at the time and in his hurry to get over the hill and control the fighting he came across D Company and **Captain Samuel Blackwell**, who had been badly wounded. Blackwell was killed sometime afterwards and is buried in Ribécourt British Cemetery. Pressing on to **Unseen Trench**, Prior discovered a number of men belonging to C Company who he scooped up in his rush for the village and quickly found himself ahead of the other three companies and the tanks:

Ribécourt was immediately in front of us. I could see parties of the enemy running through the streets. Our artillery was putting down a smoke barrage on the farther side of the village and several houses were on fire and blazing merrily. I had to decide whether to hang on in our present position and wait for the arrival of the tanks and the three other companies, or push C Company on ... I determined to take immediate action, and directed [Captain Gerald] Failes to push on at once, take the part of the village lying on this side of the ravine and hold the bridges crossing it.

By 9.00am Ribécourt had fallen, although A and C Companies met with strong opposition when clearing the village. Prior was jubilant and wrote how **Lieutenant Handcock** together with **CSM Neale** had knocked out two troublesome machine guns on the left and how the final objective of the railway station was reached by **Second Lieutenant Worn**. However, the capture of Ribécourt came at a cost to the Norfolks – 29 other ranks were killed and 58 wounded with 7 officer casualties, 3 of whom were killed.

If Ribécourt was relatively easy to take, Flesquières was a different matter altogether. The captured men of 36th Division (see general description and context section in **Route 1**) had placed the Germans at Havrincourt and Flesquières on alert. The position at Flesquières was already a strong one but to be on the safe side 3rd Battalion of IR84 had been moved forward from Noyelles together with the seasoned troops of RIR27. Artillery support was provided by FAR213 and FAR108 with elements of the Landwehr FAR282. FAR108 had already encountered French tanks on the Aisne and had received special training in using their guns against tanks.

Leaving from **Trescault**, the 51st (Highland) Division, under the command of **Major General George Harper** were tasked with the capture of Flesquières on 20 November. 152 Brigade was on the right, supported by thirty-five tanks from E Battalion, 153 Brigade was supported by thirty-five tanks from D Battalion on the left

Major General George Harper.

and remaining at Metz until called forward to continue the advance beyond Flesquières was 154 Brigade.

Directions to start: If you are approaching Ribécourt from the south on the D89, you will pass Ribécourt British Cemetery on the right before entering the village. The Grand Ravine is 200m further on. From the north Ribécourt is best approached from the direction of Flesquières. The bridge is on the D89 at Ribécourt, south of the church, drive slowly as it is easy to miss the green iron railings. Park opposite the bridge.

Route description: It is probably best to visit **Ribécourt British Cemetery** at the conclusion of the tour. We do not visit **Ribécourt Railway Cemetery**, which is just off the D29, and begun in October 1918 by the 3rd Division. The Railway Cemetery contains fifty-three 1918 burials with the exception of one man who was killed in 1916. We begin the route ❶ by the bridge captured by C Company, 9/Norfolks, the second bridge is across the fields to the west, some 300m away on the D29. You are standing on the **Grand Ravine**, which we first saw at **Grand Ravine British Cemetery**, Havrincourt. Maps and aerial photographs suggested that it was nothing more than a narrow stream – Le Riot – flowing in a broad valley, but it still conjured

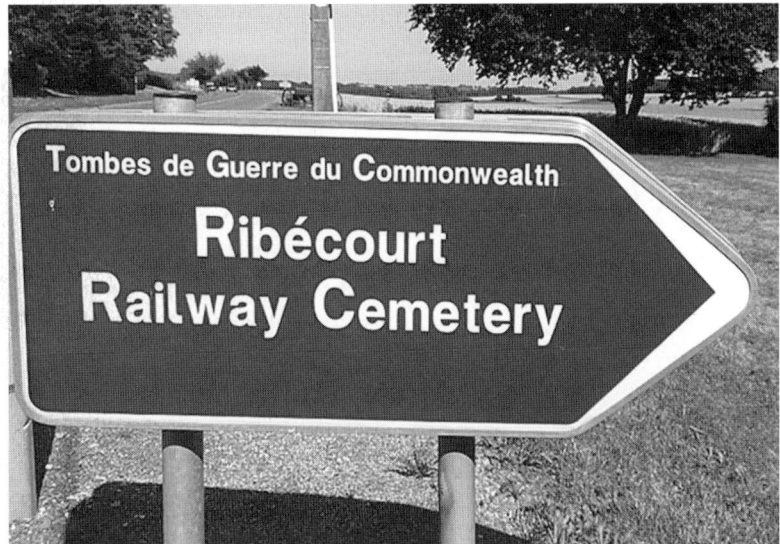

Ribécourt Railway Cemetery is well signposted.

anxiety amongst the tank crews whose job was to cross it. It was in the Grand Ravine that the infantry and tanks halted and **Second Lieutenant Horace Birks**, commanding *Double Dee II* of D Battalion, was convinced this pause had a detrimental effect on his company of tanks by giving the Germans 'forty minutes to pull themselves together'. Birks remained in the army after the Armistice and eventually retired as a major general in 1946. This was where the cavalry waited after Ribécourt had fallen and learned that Flesquières was not in British hands. Fortunately there was no mass cavalry charge up the hill and after much buck-passing between IV Corps and the 1st Cavalry Division

Horace Birks as a major general in 1944.

only **Lieutenant Arthur Tutt** and his unit of King Edward's Horse probed the German defences at Flesquières. *Leutnant* Möhring of the 108/Pioneer Company described the encounter: 'Two squadrons of English cavalry came riding towards us north east of Flesquières, all on beautiful black horses with white blazes. We let them come to within 150m and then opened up with machine gun fire. They immediately turned tail and rushed away in a wild flight with heavy loss.'

Head towards the church at Ribécourt and stop. The building is surrounded by a wide, open space and the steeple was loopholed by the defending German infantry with a concrete platform constructed some 90ft above the ground. Ribécourt had a maze of underground shelters and catacombs, probably accessed from the church which was used as a hospital. It is also said that the Germans had built a telephone exchange and electricity generator in one of them and several galleries were equipped with rails which carried small wagons. Constructed in the Middle Ages, many towns and villages in Cambrésis were located over deep excavations and continue to be natural refuges right up until the Second World War. It is, however, doubtful that the Germans, or indeed the British, knew the full extent of them.

By this time the German infantry had recovered from their initial shock and were putting up a stout defence but were unable to

The church at Ribécourt.

prevent the 11/Essex, commanded by **Lieutenant Colonel Charles Dumbell**, from passing through the Norfolks and advancing east of Flesquières towards Marcoing.

Continue uphill on the D89 and stop at the five-way intersection. **Lance Corporal Robert McBeath** won the Victoria Cross at the edge of the village on the road to the left. Continue towards Flesquières and stop by the collection of farm buildings on the left at the exit and entry point for heavy goods vehicles ❷.

This is the site of the former railway station and the Blue Line, the line of the former track line being seen to the left and right of the road. At one point Lieutenant Colonel Dumbell had a temporary headquarters in the railway station and it was here that **Second Lieutenant Worn** of the 9/Norfolks was the first to reach his battalion's objective. **Captain Daniel Hickey** must have passed through the southeast corner of the village

Lance Corporal Robert McBeath VC.

with H.28 *Hadrian*, H.27 *Hermosa* and H.29 *Havoc II* and close to what is now Ribécourt Railway Cemetery on the D29 before encountering the railway embankment to your right. He describes the scene:

> We were separated [from our objective] by the embankment of the railway running from Marcoing to Ribécourt. In descending a steep slope on to a light railway on the near side of the main line, our tank bumped heavily, and its fascine broke lose at the back and fell off. We crossed the Hindenburg Support System on the near side of the railway, keeping on the road across which the trenches had not been dug.

Hickey, on finding the trench deserted, released a pigeon to say he had reached the railway and clattered off in the direction of Marcoing.

From the former railway station the road rises to a well-defined ridge on which stands the village of Flèsquières. We are now on the eastern edge the of the 51st Division's battlefield with the 63rd Division advancing on their left and units of the 6th Division moving up on the right of the village. Flèsquières was defended initially by *Major* Fritz Hoffmeister, commanding IR84, an officer who was killed early in the battle, command devolving to *Major* Eric Krebs, commander of RIR27. Shortly before 10.00am the 1/6 Gordon Highlanders, commanded by 27-year-old **Lieutenant Colonel William Frazer**, were at the railway embankment, a short distance from the outpost line of the Hindenburg Support System. Ahead of Frazer were twelve tanks of E Battalion and as they reached the top of the hill, advancing in line ahead, the German artillery opened fire. We can get quite close to the scene of the action by taking the small track on the right of the D89 ❸, about 500m from the former railway station. Turn right along this track for 200m and, facing Flèsquières, stop. It was in these fields in front of you that the tanks of E Battalion came under fire. The tanks had moved up towards Flèsquières from the railway embankment along the line of **Chemin des Vaches**, advancing in 'line ahead' instead of their usual 'abreast' manner and we know that they crossed the Ribécourt–Flesquières road, as **Second Lieutenant Llewellyn's** tank, *Extinguisher II*, hit the paved road so hard it broke a track. It appeared that after crossing the road the 15/ Company tanks were too occupied with the machine-gun nests and failed to observe the guns of the German battery which had already got them in their sights. Unbeknown to the tanks, No. 2 Battery of 108FAR was positioned about 300m southeast of Flesquières Hill British Cemetery almost in the centre of the field, consisting of four

77mm guns (in some accounts this is described as No. 8 Battery). It was this battery and No. 3 Battery, north of the cemetery, that picked off the tanks of E Battalion as they topped the rise leading into the village. The whole area between this track and the wood was littered with burning tanks, and just behind the strip of trees jutting out from the main wood around the chateau, are the demolished remains of two German machine-gun posts which undoubtedly added to the weight of fire being directed at the attacking force. **Second Lieutenant Wilfred Bion**, commanding E.40 *Edward II*, was in the second wave of tanks but was forced to evacuate into a nearby trench when an explosion rocked the rear end: 'We were under fire, but I had not the slightest idea where the bullets were coming from. They were in fact converging on us from all directions. I told O'Toole to take charge of the trench while I tried to deal with our tormentors.'

Second Lieutenant Wilfred Bion.

From the top of his tank Bion proceeded to spray the wall of the chateau and expressed some surprise that a party of German troops, led by an officer, were pouring out of a gap in the wall and swinging round to fire at them, his gun jammed at the vital moment. What followed was a series of rushes with the two unwounded members of his crew into a trench occupied by the 1/6 Seaforth Highlanders. Bion was recommended for the award of the Victoria Cross which was downgraded to the DSO, but he had assumed command of a unit of the 6/Seaforth Highlanders after their officer, **Captain George Edwards**, had been killed in front of him. Bion went on to become an influential British psychoanalyst and was president of the British Psychoanalytical Society from 1962–5 and died in 1979.

Some German accounts state that the 2nd and 3rd Batteries between them dealt with at least eight tanks, others give the number as six and there is little doubt that the guns were being served by men who were in the locality. However, what is clear is that sixteen tanks were destroyed by direct hits on the eastern edge of Flesquières and, in total, twenty-eight of E Battalion's tanks had been ditched, disabled or suffered from mechanical breakdown. As for the small number of D Battalion tanks, it seems highly likely that they were drawn towards the east side of the village with the E Battalion tanks. D.51 *Deborah*, commanded by **Second Lieutenant Frank Heap**, continued up the D89 and actually made it into the village, coming to grief on **Rue du Calvaire**, possibly at the hands of No. 9 Battery 213FAR. Heap and the remaining men made it back to British lines, a feat that resulted in the award of the MC.

D.43 *Delysia*, under the command of **Second Lieutenant Harold Robinson**, fortunately broke down on the German first-line trench whilst D.48 *Dollar Princess*, commanded by **Second Lieutenant John McNiven**, crossed the main Hindenburg Support Line and was heading for the support

Second Lieutenant Frank Heap.

trench in front of Flesquières when he suffered a direct hit near to where Wilfred Bion had come to grief. With the tanks on fire in front of them and the crews struggling to escape, the 1/6 Gordons were pinned down by machine-gun fire and rifle fire from the machine-gun positions in and around the chateau walls. In the circumstances Lieutenant Colonel Frazer had little choice but to order his men to dig in.

Almost as soon as the fighting had concluded in front of Flesquières, a tale quickly circulated about a resolute German officer or NCO who had continued to serve his guns until he was killed, thereby causing much of the havoc amongst the tanks of E Battalion. Despite being cited by Sir Douglas Haig and Hitler as typical of the stubborn defence of the village, this ridiculous story, that the Germans themselves had no knowledge of, eventually was consigned to folklore where it belonged.

Return to the main road and turn right, passing after 80m the approximate site of Second Lieutenant Llewellyn's disabled tank and continue to the crossroad of tracks ❹. To the left is Chemin des Vaches and directly opposite is the **Monument of Nations** dedicated to the Tank Corps. Turn right here passing the gates of the chateau on the left and follow the track to the junction with the D92. At the junction turn left ❺ to reach the entrance to **Flesquières Hill British Cemetery** and the Cambrai Tank Museum where you will find the

The Monument of Nations is dedicated to the Tank Corps.

remains of the tank *Deborah*, which was unearthed on the Rue de la Haut. There is plenty of parking either outside the cemetery ❻ or in the museum car park. The cemetery was begun by the 2nd Division in 1918 on the site of Flesquières Soldiers Cemetery No. 2 and holds 914 men of whom 352 are unknown. It was made up of burials from

Flesquières Hill British Cemetery and the Cambrai Tank Museum.

six other battlefield cemeteries. After the German graves were removed temporarily to **Flesquières Communal Cemetery, German Extension** they were again moved in 1924 to their final resting place at **Cambrai East (German) Cemetery**. There are at least 124 men from the 1917 battle buried here and, as you would expect, there are a number of Tank Corps casualties. **Private Joseph Cheveton** (III.B.7) and **Lance Corporal George Foot** (III.B.6) were both 20 years old when their tank D.51 *Deborah* was hit on Rue

Lance Corporal George Foot was amongst those killed in D.51 Deborah.

du Calvaire, killing them instantly. The crew, including the two privates **William Galway** (III.B.8) and **Frederick Tipping** (III.B.9), were originally buried across the road from their tank before being moved to their present resting place. All four men were killed on 20 November. For a long time it was thought that 20-year-old **Private Walter Robinson** (III.B.10) was also part of the crew of D.51 *Deborah*, particularly as he had been buried close to the others. However, it was later established that Walter had been in D.47 *Demon II*, commanded by Second Lieutenant James Vose. The identity of the fifth casualty of D.51 remains a mystery at the time of writing. **Second Lieutenant Richard Jones** (VIII.E.10) was commanding D.41 *Devil II* when he was killed on 20 November alongside his driver, **Lance Corporal Henry Monks** (VIII.E.9), near the cemetery after a direct hit disabled his tank. **Private Harvey Hunt**, aged 21 (VII.D.6), was born in Leek, Staffordshire, and originally served in the Army Ordnance Corps before transferring to G Battalion. He was killed on 21 November with **Corporal Henry Hammond** (VII.D.6) with whom he shares a grave. **Private Trevor Lawley**, aged 37 (VIII.D.5), was a married man from Upton Bishop near Ross-on-Wye and was killed on 20 November after transferring to G Battalion in early 1917. There must be many more tank corps men buried amongst the unknowns, many of them burnt beyond recognition. By far the largest number of men buried here are the fifty-two New Zealanders killed whilst crossing the Canal de Saint-Quentin at Crèvecoeur in September 1918. One of the most senior men in the cemetery is 46-year-old **Lieutenant Colonel Reginald Walker** (I.D.1) of the Royal Engineers. He was killed on 30 September 1918, possibly during the Battle of Canal du Nord, a battle that saw twelve Victoria Crosses awarded.

Ribécourt-la-Tour and Flesquières • 39

Deborah *is finally unearthed after being buried for some eighty years.*

If you go to the wall at the rear of the cemetery and look across the fields towards Chateau Farm you should be able to see the German signalling bunker built into the chateau wall.

From the cemetery turn left and continue for a few metres to the Tank Corps Museum where you will now find the re-housed Mark IV tank D.51 *Deborah*, originally buried on the Rue de la Haut. The tank was registered as an Historical French Monument on 14 September 1999 and the new building, inaugurated on 25 November 2017, will help preserve her from the elements. Leave the museum and continue along Rue du Calvaire and stop at the village green which you will see on your left ❼. At the junction with Rue de l'Église look at the brick wall where the well-known photograph of the artillery watering their horses was taken, and shrapnel and bullet marks can still be seen today. Now glance to your right up Rue de l'Église towards the church and Mairie. The rebuilt church was designed by Pierre Leprince-Ringuet (1874–1954), who was responsible for much of the rebuilding of Cambrai in 1924. Marcel Gaumont carried out sculptural work to both the interior and exterior of the church. Outside the Mairie is the village war memorial.

From the village green it is approximately 600m along **Rue de la Haut** to the communal cemetery ❽. On the way there you will pass 25 Rue de la Haut which was very close to where the tank *Deborah* was buried. Continue over the crossroads and, keeping the cemetery

The well-known photograph of artillerymen and their horses at the watering hole in Flesquières.

on your left, carry on to the end of the car park and stop. Ahead of you is the approximate site of the D Battalion disaster and the burnt-out wreck of D.45 *Destroyer II* whilst D.41 *Devil II* was on the battalion boundary to your left. To the right was D.32 *Dop Doctor II* and D.8 *Diogenes* with D.6 *Devil-May-Care* and D.11 *Dominie* by the crossroads on **Rue de Boursies**. D.28 *Drake's Drum III* was south of Rue de Boursies to the east of the track whilst D.47 *Demon II* was close to the wooded area to the south of Rue de la Haut.

The tanks of D Battalion led 153 Brigade up the hill on the left of the attack. The two attacking battalions of infantry, the 1/7 Black Watch and the 1/7 Gordon Highlanders, quickly crossed the railway embankment but as the tanks topped the rise near the cemetery they came under fire, probably from 282FAR, which had a battery sited immediately west of the village. The resulting carnage left at least eight tanks from D Battalion, the German official history noting in its usual dulcet tone the results of the battle: 'The battery defended itself successfully against the tanks, and so provided valuable flanking protection for the soldiers of Kreb's regiment (RIR27). Feldwebelleutnant Reinsch reports the guns knocked out five tanks in a very short space of time.'

Immediately ahead of you would have been D.45 *Destroyer II*, commanded by **Second Lieutenant James Macintosh**. His account

The French Communal Cemetery on Rue de la Haut.

describes a tank to his right suddenly bursting into flames before his own tank was hit and 'all around him was flame and choking vapor and the awful screaming of stricken men'. His recollection of the next few minutes was hazy but he remembers one of his crew exiting the tank:

> From the open door [of the tank] of what was now a smoking ruin crawled a terrible figure. One arm was smashed to pulp, one leg dragged; the body was soaked in blood. But the face – one whole cheek had been blown away, and through the gaping hole the tongue could be seen working feverishly over the shattered jaw. Worse still, the light in the eyes left no room for merciful doubt but that the wreck of a man was still sane.

Macintosh admits he was unable to bring himself to shoot the man and 'with a sob laid him down and turned away'. He did manage to stumble towards the shelter of the cemetery hedge with four of his men and eventually took refuge in the sunken crossroads behind the cemetery. Macintosh's section commander, who was riding in *Demon II*, was **Captain Harold Head**, a man who as a second lieutenant took part in the successful attack on Flers in 1916. Head's part in that attack is covered in *Beyond the First Day* by Cooksey and Murland.

Another tank, D.28 *Drakes Drum III*, under the command of **Second Lieutenant John Shaw**, got within 350m of a German field gun when he was called by the infantry to deal with another gun on his right:

> I decided to try and knock out this other gun. I turned in the direction indicated by the message and crossing a slight rise perceived this gun, which was an anti-tank gun in a ground emplacement. The enemy was now on either side of us and this gun in front. I advanced straight towards this gun, my idea being to ride over it and crush the emplacement.

Shaw's tank advanced to within 20m of the gun when a second shell came through the front of the cabin, stopping the engine, but miraculously the vehicle did not catch fire. Surrounded by the enemy and captured, Shaw attributed his failure to destroy the gun to not having a male tank.

The next day plans were made to take the village of Flesquières and it was Brigadier General Buchanan's 154 Brigade that was to advance through the village and on to Fontaine-Notre-Dame. A Battalion stretcher bearer **Private Frank Brooke**, of the 1/4 Seaforth Highlanders, did not relish the idea of assaulting the Flesquières Ridge, already known as a centre of resistance:

> I felt irritable and moody. My pipe failed as a solace. I had no desire to go around the company as once. My friends were not with it ... The maniacal barrage continued with its barbarous work. It was intended to be short, heavy and ferocious, keeping the 'surprise' element. Officers' whistles sounded shrilly, and 'over' we went for the most part a yelling tumultuous crowd ... From force of habit I glanced along the company's line repeatedly, seeking casualties. No one fell: it was uncanny and mystifying. There was no rattling, spitting machine guns fire as our foremost men reached the German front line and still no casualties.

The village was deserted; the Germans had withdrawn during the night, leaving the way open for the 51st Division's advance.

Keeping the communal cemetery on your right continue for 90m and bear right ❾ at the junction, in 300m you will come to the former railway embankment. This is where the tanks lined up prior to the assault on Flesquières and across which the men of the 51st Division clambered with 153 Brigade on the left and 152 Brigade on the right.

At the railway embankment turn left and as you walk along the top of the embankment, picture for a minute the lines of tanks from D and E Battalions and the men of the 51st Division waiting between here and Chemin de Vaches, which you will pass on the left some 700m further on. Continue along the embankment to the junction with the D89, which you will recognize from your journey up the hill towards Flesquières. A right turn at the junction will take you downhill to the five-way intersection in Ribécourt. Your vehicle is a mere 250m from here past the church to the bridge.

The question inevitably arises why there were so many tank casualties on 20 November? It is frequently cited that Harper encouraged his men to maintain an appreciable gap between themselves and the tanks with the result that the tanks outdistanced the infantry. However, more recent thinking focuses on the advantage had by the Germans on the low ridge that formed a naturally defensive feature and the reinforcements, which certainly swung the balance, that were rushed as a result of the prisoners taken by IR84 at Trescault.

This is probably a good moment to visit **Ribécourt British Cemetery** ⑩, which is 200m south of the village on the D89. At the conclusion of the Battle of Cambrai the cemetery remained almost on

Ribécourt British Cemetery.

the British front line and was begun by the 6th Division in November 1917. The cemetery is a mix of 1917 and 1918 burials and there are now 290 burials, of which 20 remain unknown, although 81 men are commemorated against one wall with special memorials. There is plenty of parking in the road opposite the entrance. Here you will find ten men from the 9/Norfolks who were killed on 20 November, a surprisingly low number since A and D Companies had met with strong opposition in Ribécourt and lost three officers and twenty-nine other ranks during the day. Of these only 29-year-old **Captain Samuel Blackwell** (I.B.1) of D Company, who was from Bidford-on-Avon in Warwickshire, is buried here and of the remaining two officer casualties, **Lieutenant Cyril Jones** of C Company is buried at **Fifteen Ravine British Cemetery** at Villers-Plouich and 26-year-old **Lieutenant George Dye**, who died of wounds on 21 November, is buried at Rocquigny-Equancourt British Cemetery. **Private William Bilham** (I.B.9) is one of only nine other ranks of the 9/Norfolks buried here. Serving in D Company, he was 28 years old when he was killed on 20 November. Another 71 Brigade soldier is 36-year-old **Private Walter Kirk** (Sp. Mem. B.5) who was killed on 20 November. He enlisted in Coalville, Leicestershire, and lived in nearby Moira where his name is commemorated on the Moira War Memorial and the Donisthorpe Memorial Gateway.

There are fifteen identified members of the Tank Corps buried here, mostly from E Battalion and eleven of them have special memorials. The oldest is 42-year-old Londoner **Private John Cole** (I.D.1) who was killed on 20 November serving with E Battalion. **Second Lieutenant George Testi** (Sp. Mem. A.36) was commander of E.17 *Egypt II* when he was killed on 20 November whilst crossing **Ravine Alley** on Flesquières Ridge. His tank exploded after being hit, with none of the eight-man crew surviving. **Second Lieutenant John Howells**, aged 25 (Sp. Mem. A.35), was killed on the same day commanding *Empress II*, as was 22-year-old **Second Lieutenant Thomas Wilson** (Sp. Mem. A.42) commanding *Exquisite*. He has another memorial erected by his parents in St Mary's Church, Sutton Maddock, Shropshire. **Sergeant Wilfred Staples**, aged 23 (I.D.2), died with all the crew of *Earwig* when it was hit on the Flesquières Ridge, the only tank of 13 Company, E Battalion, to have been destroyed with all its crew on 20 November. The tank's commander, **Second Lieutenant Harold Stokes**, is commemorated on the Cambrai Memorial. The youngest identified man in the cemetery is **Private Victor Willis** (I.D.18) of F Battalion, who was killed on 1 December.

Route 3

Mœuvres

A circular tour beginning at: the French monument at Boursies on the D930

Distance: 10.2km/6.3 miles
Grade: Easy
Suitable for: 🚶 🚴
Map: Cambrai-Bertincourt 2507 SB

General description and context: The primary task of the 36th Division was to capture the enemy trenches west of the Canal du Nord and south of the Bapaume–Cambrai road. Their plan of attack was to deploy two brigades east of the canal and one brigade west with a bridge across the canal to be erected on the Demicourt–Flesquières road to take the wagons and field guns. **Brigadier General Ambrose Ricardo**, commanding 109 Brigade, had his command post on the Demicourt–Havrincourt road, close to the front line. Having captured the **Spoilbank**, 109 Brigade (36th Division) moved towards the Bapaume–Cambrai road with one platoon of the 9/Royal Inniskilling Fusiliers in the bed of the dry Canal du Nord. Intersected by the Canal du Nord which ran between Mœuvres and Bourlon, the 56th (London) Division's task was to bomb their way along the Hindenburg Line trenches to the west of Mœuvres and capture **Tadpole Copse**. The 56th Division was initially outside the actual area of advance but was tasked with co-operating on the opening day by means of a feint attack and its further action was to depend on the success gained in the main operation. Both Boursies and Demicourt were behind the British front line and our route takes us to Demicourt and then crosses the D930 to Mœuvres where we visit the Communal Cemetery Extension before returning past Tadpole Copse to Boursies.

Directions to start: Boursies is a small village on the D930 easily reached from Bapaume or Cambrai. Park either near the village memorial, a French *Poilu*, painted in horizon blue standing on the top of a column, or outside the church.

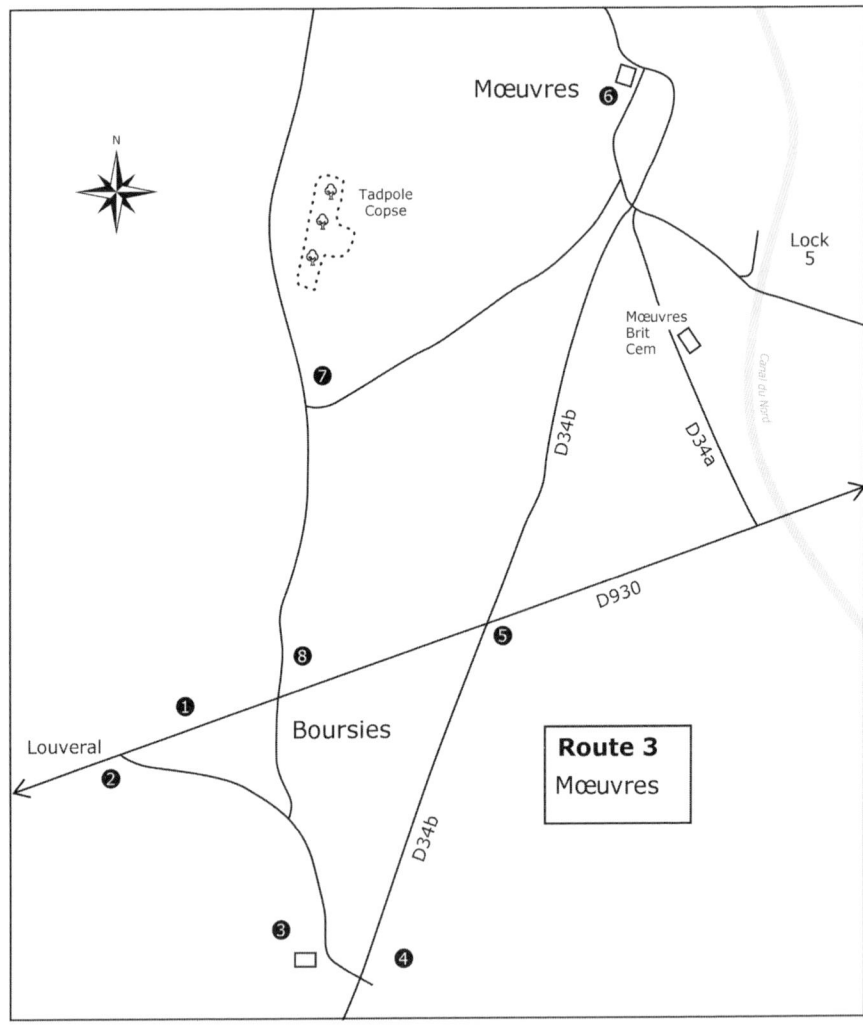

Route description: I suggest you visit the Cambrai Memorial and the attached cemetery when the route is completed. With the village war memorial and its brightly painted *poilu* ❶ on your right, continue along the D930 for 80m until you see a road on your left ❷. **Rue de Demicourt** soon leads you into open countryside and, ignoring the road to your left, Chemin de Hostein, which is marked by a stand of trees containing a calvary, continue for another 500m to **Demicourt Communal Cemetery** ❸, which you will find on your right. The British graves are on the left, just inside the gate. Prior to 1919 the cemetery contained about 100 German graves and 15 men of the 7/Argyll and Sutherland Highlanders, most of which were moved to **Hermies Hill British Cemetery**. Today the cemetery contains ten men, all of whom were killed during September and October 1918 as the BEF moved east again. A high proportion of the burials are casualties of the opening day of the Battle of the Canal du Nord on 27 September 1918, although **Second Lieutenant Henry Burton**, of Y Company 10/Duke of Cornwall's Light Infantry (DCLI), was killed by shellfire on 11 September 1918 whilst commanding 6 Platoon just south of Demicourt, his platoon of pioneers having been ordered to place blocks in the enemy trenches.

The village war memorial at Boursies.

Leave the cemetery and turning right reach the T-junction after another 200m ❹. Turn left here and walk through the village and continue until you come to a road on the right, stop here and face north towards the D930. The line of the Canal du Nord and the

Demicourt Communal Cemetery.

Hindenburg Line is to your right, as was the British front line. It was in the fields to your right that the heavy artillery of the Third Army was positioned prior to the attack on 20 November. In fact, during the German counterattack of 30 November the heavy guns were almost in the same position, as it was difficult to move the guns across no-man's-land into the Flesquières salient. Here they assisted very significantly in breaking up the German attack of 30 November. About 150m along the road to the right was **Trout Post** and it was from here that the men of 1/2 Londons (56th (London) Division) moved dummy tanks in one of two diversionary attacks towards the German lines and threw smoke bombs to convince the Germans that an assault was forthcoming. **Lieutenant Kenneth Palmer** of 513/Field Company, RE, witnessed the distraction:

> At 6.30am the whole of the artillery on the Army front opened fire on the enemy lines whilst men in the line hurled smoke bombs ahead of them to cover our movements from the line of our trenches. Then the dummy tanks were run out from cover, the dummy men were waved by others to and fro.

So realistic was the assault that the Germans blew up the road bridge crossing the Canal du Nord on the D930 which was a problem for IV Corps as they had anticipated using the crossing to bring up supplies and reinforcements! The men of 109 Brigade would have passed just east of Demicourt after the successful attack on the **Spoilbank** as they followed the line of the canal on their way north whilst the men of the 56th Division moved north through the village. Continue along the D34b towards the D930, passing over **Grayling Post** and **Support Trench** after a further 80m. At about 3.30pm the Inniskillings of 109 Brigade crossed the D930 and consolidated their position with the outpost some 300m beyond it on the D34a.

At the junction with the D930 ❺ carefully cross over and take the road directly opposite northwards, which is a continuation of the D34b. This road will take you into the village of Mœuvres. As the outskirts of the village are reached stop just before the fork in the road.

On 21 November Brigadier General Ricardo's 109 Brigade attacked between the D34b and D35a and forced their way into the southern sector of Mœuvres, protected to some degree by a smokescreen. The fighting in the village was contested yard by yard by the defending Germans of the 20th Landwehr and ID214. Every cellar and building contained enemy troops who fought bitterly to prevent the Ulstermen from capturing the village. The 9/Inniskillings reached a point where the Hindenburg Line trenches swung to the west, about 900m north of the D930. Here, heavy machine-gun fire from the vicinity of Lock 5 forced them to withdraw to where **Mœuvres British Cemetery** is situated today. On 22 November the Ulstermen of 108 Brigade relieved 109 Brigade and tried again, this time with a little more success. Managing to penetrate to the **Communal Cemetery** in the north of the village, they were forced to give ground and return to their start line in the face of strong counterattacks by the German 20th and 214th Divisions. An indication of how desperate the battle for Mœuvres became for the Germans was the fact that the infantry was led in person by the divisional commander of 214th Division, *Generalmajor* Richard von Brauchitsch. Jack Sheldon writes that the German defence was reduced to four artillery batteries drawn from three different regiments: 'It was a desperately close run affair and was almost the final contribution of the 20th Landwehr Division to the battle. Later that day, with much of its communications still cut, Headquarters 20th Landwher Division handed over command responsibility to 214th Infantry Division and moved to Douchy.'

On 23 November, supported by eleven tanks from E Battalion, 107 Brigade captured Lock 5 and the 12/Irish Rifles of 108 Brigade, in what was their last attempt to capture the village, managed to temporarily get into the village with three companies but were forced out at nightfall. Imagine if you will the shattered remains of the village and the men of the 36th Division advancing with fixed bayonets through a storm of machine guns and shellfire supported by the tanks, some of them on fire, crushing the wire and firing with their 6-pounders at the enemy.

Continue across the junction, following the D34a along the Grand Rue. **Mœuvres Communal Cemetery Extension** ❻ is 500m ahead of you on the road leading to Inchy en Artois. Pass the rebuilt church on the right and following CWGC signs the cemetery is on the left marked by a large calvary. The extension now contains 565 Commonwealth burials and commemorations, 263 of the burials are unidentified but special memorials are erected to 31 casualties known or believed to be buried amongst them. Other special memorials commemorate three casualties buried in Boursies Communal Cemetery whose graves could not be found. The cemetery also contains ninety-three war graves of other nationalities, most of them German. The cemetery was always in German hands apart from the few hours it was held by the Ulstermen. Again, it was touch and go as to whether the Ulstermen could hold on to their gains.

Mœuvres Communal Cemetery Extension.

The centre and western sector of the village had been cleared and many Germans had been killed in dugouts and cellars and, pushing on, the men of 107 Brigade took **Cemetery Support Trench** on the western fringes of the cemetery and began to consolidate. Then came the counterattack by II/88 Reserve Regiment of the 21st Division. The enemy was seen to be assembling in **Hobart Street**, to the north of the cemetery, and 40 minutes from the attack being launched, the British were driven back to the southern outskirts of the village. On the night of 25 November the 36th Division was relieved by the 2nd Division and Mœuvres would remain in German hands for the remainder of the campaign. It was partly taken by the 57th (West Lancashire) Division in September 1918 and completely cleared the next day by the 52nd (Lowland) Division. **Lieutenant Colonel Clinton Battye**, aged 43 (VI.C.25), is the most senior of the men buried here. He was killed on 24 November by a burst of machine-gun fire in a street close to his Battalion Headquarters in Bourlon village. Originally buried in the garden of the house in which he died, his body was reinterred in the communal cemetery extension sometime in 1918. As you might expect, there are a number of men from the 56th Division buried here, three of which were in the 16/Londons. **Second Lieutenant John Hooper** (Sp. Mem. F5) was serving with the 16/Londons (Queen's

Westminster Rifles) when he was killed in action on 30 November aged 26. He enlisted into the London Regiment as a private, and arrived in France on 24 January 1915 and was commissioned in December 1916. **Rifleman Stanley Bradley**, aged 25 (III.A.29), was employed by the statistical department of the Board of Trade before he enlisted into the 16/Londons. He was killed on 30 November. In the same battalion was 25-year-old **Rifleman Michael Humphry** (III.B.2). He was also killed on 30 November and left a widow, Emily. He is remembered on the war memorial in Horley.

Second Lieutenant John Hooper, 16/Londons.

There are very few of the 36th Division amongst the identified but no doubt many of them lie amongst the unknown burials. Amongst the identified is 20-year-old **Second Lieutenant Laurence Martin** (III.A.19) who was serving with the 9/RIF (North Irish Horse) when he was killed on 23 November whilst attacking Mœuvres. He was the only officer killed that day in 108 Brigade but six other officers were wounded and eighty-two other ranks were killed, wounded or missing. Killed on the same day was **Sergeant Mathew Harper** (I.D.24) serving with the 13/Royal Irish Rifles. **Captain William Fugeman**, aged 20 (VI.B.11), was serving in C Company, 23/Royal Fusiliers (99 Brigade) when he was shot in the head by a sniper near Bourlon Wood. He arrived in France in April 1916 having previously been a student at the University of London. Of the 1918 men buried here, **Lieutenant Charles Pope VC** (V.D.22) of the 11/Battalion AIF was killed in April 1917 just north of Boursies on the right flank of the Australian Battle of Bullecourt. His award of a posthumous Victoria Cross was gazetted on 8 June 1917.

From the cemetery retrace your steps along Rue d'Inchy and take the road on

Lieutenant Charles Pope VC.

the right – **Rue du Calvaire** which runs alongside the communal cemetery. Follow the road for 500m, through a right-hand bend, and take the minor road on the right. Stop here ❼. To your right are the wind turbines on the hill leading to **Tadpole Copse**, about 900m west of Mœuvres. This is the area attacked by the 56th (London) Division and the road junction which you have stopped by is a service road leading to the turbines. The copse formed a commanding tactical feature of the Hindenburg Line and was stormed on the evening of 22 November by the **16/Londons (Queen's Westminster Rifles)**. The division held on to the copse despite being attacked from all sides. Major Walter Grey, the divisional historian, wrote that the assault was far from easy:

> The severe trench fighting continued; finally at 5.30pm the QWR (Queen's Westminster Rifles) captured Tadpole Copse and began bombing forward to Tadpole Lane ... Though in the end successful, the QWR had a very trying time in capturing the copse and in withstanding frequent counterattacks that the enemy made during the night it was decided they should be relieved on the 23rd by the 1/2 Londons.

During the German counterattack of 30 November, Tadpole Copse was overrun and the division was forced back towards the old British front line.

The Cambrai Memorial at Louveral.

The Military Cemetery at Louveral.

Continue straight on. The track will take you to Boursies and was probably used by the 56th Division as they approached Tadpole Copse and, if you listen hard, you can almost hear the men of 169 Brigade marching along the roadway towards the copse. At the junction with the D930 ❽ turn right and continue along the right-hand side of the main street until you reach the zebra crossing opposite the church from where you should see your vehicle. Now is probably a good moment to visit the **Cambrai Memorial** and the **Military Cemetery at Louveral**. Drive along the D930 towards Bapaume for just over a kilometre to find the memorial on the right. There is plenty of parking.

The memorial records the names of 7,048 officers and men of the Third

Second Lieutenant Charles Hartley, 2/Coldstream Guards.

Army who died between 20 November and 3 December and who are missing and have no known grave. It was unveiled by **Sir Louis Vaughan**, the Chief of Staff to Sir Julian Byng on 4 August 1930. The names are inscribed on a semi-circular cloistered wall and on the end of the memorial are some particularly fine examples by **Charles Jagger** depicting trench life. He died in November 1934. The memorial itself was designed by **Harold Charlton Bradshaw** and stands on the same plot as the cemetery, which was begun in April 1917. Amongst the 118 identified burials are a mixture of men who were killed during 1917 and 1918 as well as 2 private memorials commemorating **Lieutenant Herbert Windeler**, 4/Grenadier Guards (see **Route 5**), and **Second Lieutenant Charles Hartley**, 2/Coldstream Guards. Both men were killed on 27 November 1917 in, or close to, Bourlon Wood.

Route 4
Graincourt-lès-Havrincourt

An out and back tour beginning and ending at: the church in Graincourt-lès-Havrincourt

Distance: 2.3km/1.4 miles
Grade: Easy
Suitable for: 🚶 🚴 🚗
Map: Cambrai-Bertincourt 2507 SB

General description and context: A short stroll on roads around Graincourt-lès-Havrincourt, hereafter referred to as Graincourt, takes the visitor to the communal cemetery and back. It is perfectly possible to complete the route by car, continuing across the motorway into Anneux and then via the D15 to the main road from where Bourlon village and wood is easily accessed.

Graincourt was captured by **Brigadier General Roland Bradford's** 186 Brigade on 20 November along with two cavalry squadrons of the 1/King Edwards Horse, who quickly discovered horses do not mix well with barbed wire and machine guns. We are told that six tanks of G Battalion were put out of action on the edge of the village by direct hits from the two German 77mm field guns. The *History of G Battalion* indicates these guns were knocked out by gunfire from two tanks from 20 and 21 Companies who then proceeded to disable the guns. One of these guns was towed away by G.29 *Gorgonzola* under the command of **Lieutenant Albert Baker** of 20 Company, and presumably this is the gun on display today at the Tank Museum at Bovington. However, there is a difference of opinion over the number of tanks involved in the capture of Graincourt, another source reporting that four sections of 21 Company were involved in the capture of the village, namely G.4 *Gloucester II*, G.5 *Glenlivet II*, G8 *Gossip II*, G.46 *Gina*, G.7 *Giggle*, G. 55 *Gadzooks*, G.26 *Goodbye-ee*, G.11 *Glamorgan*, G.9 *Gondolier* and G.23 *Germicide* (G.46 was ditched west of Graincourt and G.26 was hit but returned to base). There is no mention of G.29 except in **Captain Douglas Browne's** account in *The Tank in Action*. He writes that the guns were spotted by Charles

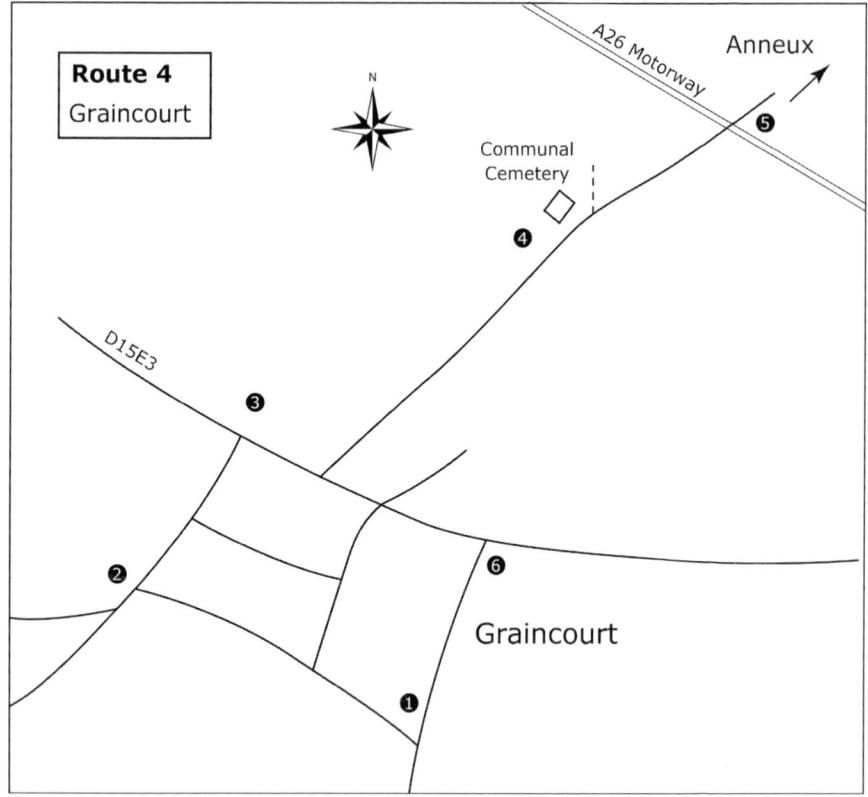

Baker by the dust thrown up after the first discharge and a few 6-pounder shells drove the gunners away and one gun was towed away by G.29. Whatever the reality, it appears that two companies of 2/4 Duke of Wellington's along with **Major Ralph Broome**, commanding 21 Company G Battalion, proceeded to overpower the guns. Broome directed three tanks and G.29 eventually accounted for their destruction. Albert Baker, the commander of G.29, later received a bar to his MC.

The continuing good progress made by 186 Brigade was due almost entirely to the drive and enthusiasm of **Brigadier General Roland Bradford**, who at 25 years old was the youngest general in the British Army. Bradford above all recognized the importance of a rapid advance, a trait that **Major General Walter Braithwaite** (62nd Division) was quick to exploit:

I decided to 'chance my arm'. I gave him instructions to keep moving forward, and directly the leading brigades had gained some initial success; the 186 Brigade should push through. It was taking a bit of a risk, but if it came off it was well worth it. As a matter of fact it did come off and had a tremendous effect on the fortunes of the day. Bradford was a born leader and led his brigade with conspicuous success.

Bradford was already the holder of the Victoria Cross and his older brother, 31-year-old **Lieutenant Commander George Bradford**, was also awarded a posthumous Victoria Cross at Zeebrugge in April 1918. **Captain Thomas Bradford**, the oldest brother, survived the war but **Second Lieutenant James Bradford**, an officer with 18/Durham Light Infantry (DLI), died of wounds in May 1917. Roland Bradford was killed seventeen days after he was given command of 186 Brigade.

With the guns neutralized, the tanks then drove up the main street and the infantry took Graincourt by 3.30pm with posts established on the northern edge of the village near the communal cemetery. Before dusk 186 Brigade troops pushed forward to Anneux but withdrew as darkness prevented any 'mopping up' of German troops. Nevertheless, B and D Companies of the 2/4 Duke of Wellington's occupied the sugar factory on the D930 and then advanced towards the quarry and chapel at Anneux assisted by a tank. The quarry was occupied by IR175 and their post was reported to have been crushed by the tank. The 186 Brigade war diary tells us that Bradford and his staff used the sunken road close to the Communal Cemetery in Graincourt as its headquarters on the night of 20 November, not moving into the catacombs beneath the church until 21 November. The next morning three German electricians were taken prisoner in the catacombs and not released until they demonstrated how the electric plant functioned! 186 Brigade entered Anneux in the face of heavy machine-gun fire from the men of RIR52. Various accounts tell us that the attack was supported by up to twenty tanks from F Battalion with two squadrons of dismounted cavalry in addition to **Lieutenant Colonel Roland Anderson's** 11/Hussars. Apart from one tank of F Battalion, the remainder reached their objective whilst six tanks from 19 Company G Battalion and six from 21 Company attacked their objective without loss. By 2.10pm the village had been cleared of enemy troops.

Directions to start: Graincourt is best approached from the D630 from where the D15E3 leads straight into the village. If approaching from the south, the best route is via Flesquières using the D89, passing **Orival Wood British Cemetery**, turn onto the D15E3 which will take you into the village. Park in the village square near the Marie on Rue de l'Église.

Route description: The route begins by the war memorial. Before you begin find the entrance to the catacombs which lie beneath the church ❶ at Graincourt, the entrance is by a small doorway at the side of the building. Surveyed by Monsieur Gilbert with the help of pupils from École Publique Gouzeaucourt, the catacombs have been found to be extensive, although today these are mainly bricked up. It was to the safety of these ancient workings that Brigadier General Bradford moved his Brigade Headquarters staff on 21 November from the cemetery in Graincourt. By the time Bradford's 186 Brigade had captured the village the church was a ruin but today the entrance to the catacombs is via a small doorway.

From the church, which you should keep on your right, proceed up **Rue de l'Église**. As you head towards the junction with **Rue d'Hermies** ❷ glance to your left towards the open fields, this may well have been the position of the two German field guns that scored direct hits on at least six British tanks. At the junction turn right into **Rue des Guensses** for 120m until another road junction is reached ❸. Stop here. Local information recounts how the British tanks of G Battalion used the line of this road as they swept through the village. Just imagine the confusion as the troops of 186 Brigade advanced in the face of the 20th Landwehr Division through these streets. Turn right at the junction and as you do look to the left along **Rue Dainville**. This

The war memorial at Graincourt.

L'Église Saint-Martin at Graincourt.

road leads directly to the former sugar factory and was probably used by the 2/4 Dukes on 20 November and the 14/HLI and 12/Suffolks on 23 November. (See **Route 6**.) After 60m turn left along **Rue de la Chapelle**, this minor road, signposted to Anneux, leads directly to the cemetery.

Arriving at the cemetery ❹ stop and look at the layout of the ground. Running alongside the cemetery is a sunken track, which today finishes by the motorway but in 1917 continued north to meet to main road some 300m east of the motorway. Bradford either established his headquarters in the trees on the right of the cemetery, which would have provided cover from aerial observation, or in the sunken track which runs alongside. It is evident that the forward position occupied by Bradford at Graincourt must have been partly responsible for the rapid advance made by 186 Brigade and it is interesting to contrast him with Erwin Rommel in the Second World War, who adopted forward positions in his successful 1940 campaign.

Continue to the bridge across the A26 motorway, Anneux lies before you ❺. This is the furthest point reached in **Route 4** but if you are travelling in a vehicle you can continue over the motorway into Anneux itself.

The battle for the Anneux was violent and costly. German rifleman lured their opponents into the village and then fired on them from

The communal cemetery at Graincourt.

the upper storeys and attic windows of the buildings, much the same as they did in Bourlon. But the weight of fire was against the Germans and by mid-afternoon on 21 November the 12/Company of RIR52 was down to twenty surviving men and with the advancing F Battalion tanks making headway, *Leutnant* Weßlau was relying on artillery to deal with them. He was mistaken:

> We observed flashes in amongst the tanks and thought at first that they were the impacts of our artillery. We soon discovered, however, that they were the flashes of the tanks firing their own guns, seemingly completely at random. As the tanks drew closer, a lot of fire passed very close to us, but they did not enjoy much success. However, it was really unpleasant when one of the tanks crossed and re-crossed our line, engaging us at point blank range with main armament and machine gun fire ... unfortunately a tank made us aware once more of the seriousness of our situation. This beast drove systematically along our lines, causing Thomas's platoon heavy casualties.

Anneux remained in Allied hands until 6 December and was recaptured by the British on 27 September 1918.

The return journey takes you back down the Rue de la Chapelle to the junction where a left turn will take you into Rue de Marcoing. Turn right again into Rue Saint-Joseph ❻, your vehicle is by the war memorial some 200m away.

Route 5

Cantaing-sur-Escaut and Fontaine-Notre-Dame

A circular tour beginning and ending at: Cantaing-sur-Escaut

Distance: 8.1km/5.7 miles
Grade: Easy
Suitable for: 🚶 🚴
Map: Cambrai-Bertincourt 2507 SB

General description and context: There were three assaults on Fontaine-Notre-Dame, hereafter known as Fontaine, the first two delivered by the 51st (Highland) Division and the third by the Guards Division. Our route focuses mainly on the assaults by the 51st Division but does refer to the Guards attack of 27 November and the D142, where two Victoria Crosses were won by **Sergeant John McAuley** of the 1/Scots Guards on 27 November and another by **Lance Corporal John Thomas** of 2/5 North Staffordshires, 59th (North Midland) Division, on 30 November.

After finding Flesquières deserted by German troops early on 21 November, 154 Brigade advanced on **Cantaing-sur-Escaut**, hereafter known as Cantaing, with the 4/Gordon Highlanders covering the front of 152 Brigade and the 7/Argyll and Sutherland Highlanders covering 153 Brigade. Bringing up the rear on the right was the 1/9 Royal with the 1/4 Seaforth Highlanders on the left. The **Cantaing Line** presented a formidable set of obstacles and foremost amongst them of all was the double belt of wire some 15m in depth. The attack was due to begin at 10.00am and the men of 154 Brigade halted to await the arrival of the tanks, which only made an appearance some 2 hours later; in fact, the tanks of B Battalion were being refitted at **Premy Chapel** and were obviously not in a position to respond to the 51st Division's attack. Unable to wait any longer for the tanks of B Battalion, **Brigadier General Kenneth Buchanan** ordered 154 Brigade to continue the advance. Although the rain obscured the German observers in Bourlon Wood, the

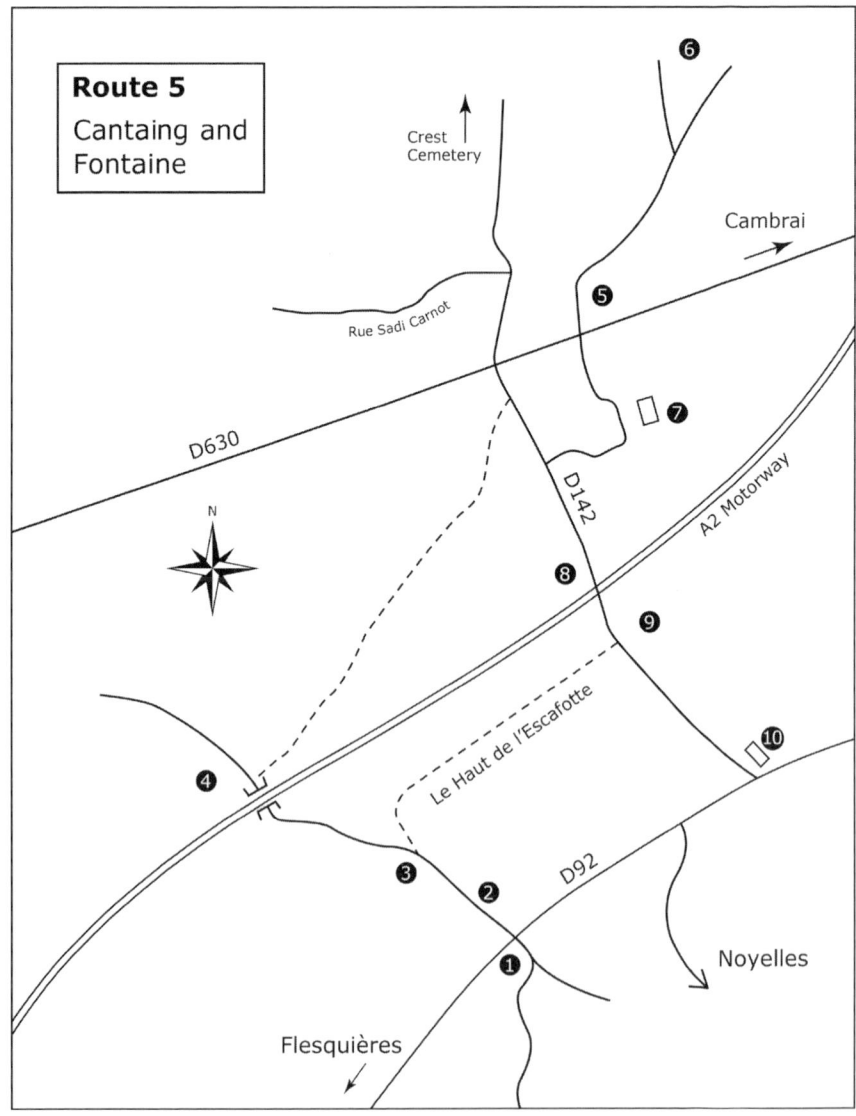

Highlanders were soon held up short of the village by the weight of fire being directed by the two regiments of IR107, which had been rushed into position during the night to reinforce IR52 and RIR232. Just after midday thirteen tanks of B Battalion arrived, although in some accounts there is confusion about the actual number that turned up. Depending on which version you read, the number of tanks is put at seven or ten and there was even an account of four tanks of B Battalion being 'discovered' in **Nine Wood** by the 2/Dragoon Guards. However, by noon tanks were making good progress into the village, but were reported to be unsupported by any infantry and anxious about the fate of his tanks in the village, **Lieutenant Colonel Edward Bryce**, commanding B Battalion, sent a request for assistance to **Brigadier General Ernest Makins**, commanding 1st Cavalry Brigade. In response, all three squadrons of the 2/Dragoon Guards moved north along the canal and galloped the village from the east, and by 1.40pm the village was reported clear of enemy.

Meanwhile, in the southwestern corner of the village at **Cantaing Mill** the Germans continued to resist and once again the Highlanders were brought to a halt by intense machine-gun fire. Despite two Stokes mortars being brought into action, it was not until 3.00pm that one of the tanks en route for Fontaine finally cleared the pocket of resistance, the surviving Germans escaping to **La Folie Wood**. It was just as well as H.30 *Hydra* and H.25 *Harlequin* had already been put out of action on the road running from La Justice to Cantaing by the two field guns at **Cantaing Mill**.

On 23 November there was a combined attack on Bourlon Wood and Fontaine with two battalions of 152 Brigade detailed to assault Fontaine along with tanks from H, B and C Battalions. In the centre of the action the thirteen tanks from B Battalion and six from C Battalion led the attack with the 1/6 Gordon Highlanders approaching the village from the west. The main problem was anti-aircraft guns mounted on the backs of lorries (*K Flak*), two of these lorries, commanded by *Hauptmann Haehner* and *Leutnant* Zorn, being responsible for the destruction of seven tanks of B Battalion of which only three, B.14 *Bella Donner*, B.19 *Beach Comber* and B.35 *Bogey II*, managed to get back to their base at Marcoing. In the afternoon a renewed attack by 1/5 Seaforths supported by twelve tanks from I Battalion entered the village in darkness, although some reports say it was only nine. The failure of both assaults has been put down to the fact there were only two battalions from 152 Brigade involved in the attack and there were at least four other battalions of the 51st Division available to assist. The notion of the 51st Division's practice of leaving a considerable gap between the tanks and infantry raised its head again but on this occasion the infantry's progress was certainly blocked by machine-gun fire from the buildings on the edge of the village, leaving the tanks stranded and taking the fire from the *K-Flak* guns. The jury is still out on whether or not this contributed to the failure of the 51st Division at Fontaine. During the night of 23–24 November the division was relieved by the Guards Division.

Byng decided to make one more effort on 27 November to try to recapture Fontaine and Bourlon Wood, despite the reservations of divisional commander **Major General Fielding**, in charge of the Guards Division, who described the idea as 'a dangerous and impracticable undertaking for which there could be no kind of justification'. The attack commenced at 6.20am on 27 November 1917 with the 3/Grenadier Guards heading for Fontaine supported by fourteen tanks and no heavy artillery barrage. The machine-gun fire was heavier than expected with **Captain Harold Dearden**, the medical officer attached to the Grenadiers, describing it as sounding like one continuous scream:

> The Boche put down a terrific barrage too, and our poor lads went down like grass before a reaper. They kept steadily on though, and we reached the village on time. I got a good many walking wounded back, but the fire was hopeless for the [stretcher] bearers, and I had half of them knocked out before the village was reached.

Once in Fontaine there followed intense street fighting but by 8.30am most of Fontaine had been taken by the Guards including the church and the area around railway station. Having sustained heavy losses, however, and in the face of a German counterattack starting at 10.00am the British were forced to retreat to their starting lines. The losses amongst the Guards were dreadful. Of the 1,350 men that formed the 3 attacking battalions, only 200 Grenadiers, 180 Coldstream and 80 Irish Guards returned to the start line. Amongst the dead was **Lieutenant Gavin Bowes-Lyon**, 3/Grenadier Guards, a first cousin of the future Queen Elizabeth II; he is commemorated on the Cambrai Memorial.

Directions to start: Cantaing can be approached from the direction of Cambrai taking the D142 in Fontaine-Notre-Dame and from Marcoing using the D29 through Noyelles. On arrival at your destination park your vehicle at the western end of the village where the D92 passes a small triangular green on its way to Flesquières. There is plenty of parking around the green and it is marked by a signpost at one end directing you to Noyelles, Fontaine and Cambrai. If you pass the water tower on Rue de Graincourt as you exit the village, you have gone too far.

Route description: It is possible to shorten the route by turning right at Cantaing Mill and continuing along **Le Haut de l'Escafotte** to the D149 where a right turn will bring you back into Cantaing (4.2km/2.6 miles). Either way, from the green ❶ cross the D92 and continue straight ahead along **Rue d'Anneux**. After a few metres you will pass the memorial to Ewart Mackintosh, stop here ❷. The emblem of the Seaforth Highlanders stands proudly nearby and on the back wall of the chapel are information boards containing further information about Mackintosh. From the chapel continue along the road and stop at the junction.

Ewart Mackintosh, the war poet, who is remembered in the chapel at Cantaing.

A small track runs to the right of the road, this is the former site of **Cantaing Mill** ❸ which apart from the machine guns and a heavy trench mortar, contained two 77mm field guns and was heavily wired. The mill must have enveloped the whole of the junction and clearly had a wide field of fire, for it was during the attack by D Company of the 1/4 Gordon Highlanders that the poet **Lieutenant Ewart**

The chapel dedicated to Ewart Mackintosh at Cantaing.

The back wall of the chapel at Cantaing.

Mackintosh, serving with 1/4 Seaforth Highlanders, was killed whilst the battalion was advancing into Cantaing. The Seaforths were moving up to the left of the water tower on the D92. It is highly possible that **Private Frank Brooke** of the 1/4 Seaforth Highlanders witnessed his death:

> The enemy had to be cleared from the village. We commenced the attack crawling up the slope, seeking depressions in the ground for shelter, then away again, in spasmodic rushes. I saw the company commander, Lieutenant Macintosh [sic], lent to us from the Fifth Battalion, get a bullet between the eyes. He stood bolt upright and paid the penalty for such foolishness.

At the junction ignore the right turn, which is part of the short route, and continue until the track goes over the motorway ❹. It is likely that the 1/7 Argyll and Sutherland Highlanders and the 1/4 Seaforths cut this corner of the route and made their way directly across country from Cantaing Mill. This is also the route the tanks of H Battalion would have taken on their way to Fontaine. We will have to cross the A2 motorway via the bridge before we turn right where the road soon deteriorates into a track and heads northeast into Fontaine. From this track there are good views of the dark mass of Bourlon Wood which can be seen to your left with the church spire of Fontaine to its right.

The tanks of H Battalion probably entered the village along Rue de Flesquières and were the first British troops to enter Fontaine, H.23 *Hong Kong*, H.27 *Hermosa*, H.28 *Hadrian* and H.29 *Havoc II* charged the village with guns blazing, wheeling right along the main street silencing the machine guns. **Captain Daniel Hickey**, commanding 7 Section, remembered entering the village without the infantry and feeling quite alone:

Captain Daniel Hickey.

Twilight was falling and there was a mist rising from the ground as we reached the outskirts of the village, which we scoured for half an hour without seeing any enemy. Cambrai was only two miles away – and the gate to it was ours! The tank commanders all told of a shortage of petrol and ammunition; the male tanks had practically come to the end of their 200 rounds each of 6-pounder shells; the engines of the tanks were running hot because of thin oil; and the crews were exhausted. If the infantry failed to turn up what orders should I give?

Fortunately the infantry turned up and Hickey's tanks left the village and returned, cutting across country to **Orival Wood** (see **Route 10**). The infantry advanced from Cantaing under heavy fire from rifles and machine guns but the advance of some 4,000m under concentrated rifle fire had sadly depleted the Highlanders and No. 1 Company, 1/4 Seaforths, lost its commander, 24-year-old **Captain 'Ray' Macdonald**, who fell whilst 300–400yd from Fontaine. Of his company, which had started out that morning with 125 men, only 40 were left, but by 5.00pm Fontaine was in British hands and the village was prepared for an all-round defence. Incredibly, at 8.00pm the three companies of Argyll and Sutherland Highlanders were withdrawn and, although it was later maintained this was to place the

A line drawing of Lieutenant Colonel John Unthank in later life.

defence of the village under 42-year-old **Lieutenant Colonel John Unthank** of the 1/4 Seaforths, it sadly reduced the strength of the defending Highlanders, the whole of the Seaforths only mustering 140 fighting men. The Scots had made a start on clearing the cellars but there was still a large number of Germans hiding below ground and at least a dozen enemy aircraft circled over the village and though the headquarters staff drove them higher with their rifle fire, they continued to dive on unsuspecting Scotsmen and persisted with their observation.

Continue for 80m to the main road and turn right, passing the CWGC signpost for **Crest Cemetery** on the left. Stop here. If you continue north along the D140 for 400m you will eventually come to **Rue Sadi Carnot** on the left where the water tower marks the beginning of the unmetalled road to Bourlon through the wood. You will also find the memorials to **Lieutenants Hartley and Windler**, both killed during the Guards attack on Fontaine on 27 November.

Where you are standing is probably on the route taken by the tanks of H Battalion as they entered the village on 21 November and where F.41 *Fray Bentos II* was hit on 23 November. Turn right along the Route National and in 200m turn left along **Rue Roger**

Crest Cemetery.

The former railway station at Fontaine.

Salengro ❺, bearing right along **Rue de la République** to the five-way intersection. At the intersection take Avenue de la Gare for 90m to find the former railway station building on the right ❻. The building was held by Lieutenant Colonel Unthank for a time and it was from here that Unthank and his sadly depleted battalion probably arranged to defend the village. On 27 November the railway station and line were again captured by the 1/Coldstream Guards but their hold was tenuous, in fact the station was lost and then regained before their position was driven in. There are reports of only one officer and fifteen men managing to escape from being taken prisoner.

Lieutenant Colonel Unthank was never destined to hold onto Fontaine and despite placing four machine guns on all the exits to the village, the next day saw a German attack with ID119, IR58 and IR46 along the whole line, enveloping both flanks. The Germans poured out of the trees bordering Bourlon and charged down the hillside whilst others advanced from the **Folie Wood** direction, the attack coming in five waves at ten-pace intervals, forcing the depleted Seaforths to abandon Fontaine after heavy fighting. **Lieutenant Macdonnell**, who was the Artillery Liaison Officer with the battalion, described the final moments in typically jocular tones:

> We loosed off the remainder of our stuff [ammunition] at them, and then, hotly pursued, we bunked off across the fields with

hundreds of shots at us. How we ran for about 1000 yards! But we had not many casualties ... Altogether it was a wonderful show, but it was an awful pity that we ran out of ammunition. The CO, on the left, fought to the last gasp, and was surrounded by half a dozen Huns, who told him to surrender. He seized a rifle and went for them club fashion, bald headed, laid some out and got away. The Adjutant fought to the end, but was wounded in the leg and taken prisoner.

Now retrace your steps to the junction of **Rue Roger Salengro** with the main road and, crossing straight over, continue along **Rue de la Liberté** to the church. Behind the church is a small road leading directly to the cemetery, please make an effort to visit the three headstones just inside the gate, against the wall, two are unidentified Seaforth Highlanders and the third is completely unknown ❼. On 23 November, during the second assault on Fontaine, Rue de la Liberté

L'Église Saint-Martin at Fontaine.

Cantaing-sur-Escaut and Fontaine-Notre-Dame • 71

The entrance to the communal cemetery at Fontaine.

became the scene of a dramatic rescue between the disabled tank C.47 *Conqueror II* and C.48 *Caesar*. Hit by a unit of RIR52 using armour-piercing ammunition, C.47 was brought to a halt near the church with its commander, **Second Lieutenant Willie Moore**, seriously

The three solitary graves in the communal cemetery. The church can be seen behind.

The modern motorway bridge close to the pumping station on the D142.

wounded. C.48 stopped near the wreck and, despite being under enemy fire, **Private Green** got out and helped evacuate *Conqueror II's* crew and **Private Raffel** assisted the wounded Moore. Only when all eight crew members were safely on board did C.48's commander, **Second Lieutenant Archibald**, give the order to leave. For this action Archibald and Moore received the Military Cross, Green the DCM and Raffel the MM.

From the cemetery road turn left for 70m and then take the right turn into **Rue Paul Bert** which will take you back to the D142. Turn right towards Cantaing, but take care along here as speeding traffic is always a possibility. The D142 is the sunken road along which **Lieutenant Hon. Arthur Kinnard** took D Company of the 1/Scots Guards towards Fontaine on 27 November and where he was mortally wounded on the Fontaine side of the motorway bridge, about 400m short of the modern pumping

John McAuley VC survived the war and returned to the Glasgow police and was promoted to sergeant.

station. **Sergeant John McAuley** then took his company commander back to the safety of a dugout and took charge of the company, beating off several German attacks and leaving some fifty Germans dead. For this feat he was awarded the **Victoria Cross** ❽. Kinnard is buried at **Ruyaulcourt Military Cemetery**. To your left is **Folie Wood** from where numerous machine guns directed their fire onto the troops moving along the D142; the wood was never taken by the British during the first Cambrai offensive.

Lance Corporal John Thomas VC, 2/5 North Staffordshires.

Just left of the road, on the Cantaing side of the motorway bridge and to the north of the junction of **Le Haut de l'Escafotte** with the D142, was the scene of another **Victoria Cross** action on 30 November by **Lance Corporal John Thomas** of the 2/5 North Staffordshires ❾. Battalion Headquarters was at Cantaing Mill and, observing the enemy preparing for another assault from the direction of Folie Wood, Thomas ran forward

Cantaing British Cemetery.

across the road to a dugout which was used by the Germans to concentrate their troops. Shooting three snipers and dealing with the Germans in the dugout, he returned, bringing back valuable information on enemy dispositions enabling the artillery to break up the attack. To get closer to the scene of the action take the track on the left of the road and continue parallel to the road until you are about 100m from the motorway. Thomas won his cross in the fields to your right.

Continue towards Cantaing and stop at Staffords ⑩. This is a small cemetery on a roadside bank just to the left of the junction of the D142 with the D92. There are sixty-eight headstones of which five are unknown. All of the men here were killed in September and October of 1918 and, although not often visited, the cemetery contains some quite remarkable individuals, not least of whom is 24-year-old **Captain Patrick Lavelle** of the 1/5 Royal Scots Fusiliers who was killed on 4 October 1918. Twice Mentioned in Despatches, this Lanarkshire man was also awarded the **Croix de Guerre with Palm**. He sailed from Liverpool in May 1915 for Gallipoli where the battalion disembarked in June.

Leave the cemetery, turning right along the main street of Cantaing and ignoring the road to Noyelles on the left, stop at the church. Two tanks of B Battalion are said to have been destroyed here but not before they had set the church tower ablaze and dealt with a

The church at Cantaing.

Cantaing-sur-Escaut and Fontaine-Notre-Dame • 75

machine-gun position. However, the British did not have everything their own way. *Unteroiffizer* Feldweg, a platoon commander with the 6th Company, RIR232, was responsible for destroying two tanks, but whether these are the two tanks of B Battalion remains unknown:

> I asked for several grenades to be passed to me. Joining them together into one large charge I made my way towards one of the tanks. I made a quick decision then threw the entire charge at the tank. There was a mighty explosion then the tank disappeared behind a great cloud of black smoke. About twenty minutes later I went back to it. The charred corpses of its crew lay there. I then observed the British were employing the second tank. I did not delay but prepared a second charge, crept up behind it to throwing range and hurled the charge unto the tank which tore its petrol tank off. We took the entire crew prisoner.

From the church it is 450m back to your vehicle.

Route 6

Bourlon

A circular tour beginning at: the shrine at les Trois Cornets

Distance: 7.5km/4.6 miles
Grade: Easy
Suitable for: 🚶 🚲
Map: Cambrai-Bertincourt 2507 SB

General description and context: The hard facts of the matter were: unless Bourlon Ridge was captured the British would be forced to withdraw. Sir Douglas Haig was between a rock and a hard place, the ridge would have to be taken quickly, but a properly coordinated attack would take a day or two, and in that time the Germans would have enough time to recover. The weather was appalling, cold, wet, with sleet and some snow on the ground, and not conducive to fighting. Such weather had a detrimental effect on conditions on the ground and Bourlon Wood suffered terribly. Mud and impenetrable undergrowth amongst the densely wooded area added to the woes of the men of both sides as they struggled in wet, mud-caked uniforms. How they managed to fight in such circumstances is hard to believe.

In this brief summary the attacks on Bourlon and the British movements in the wood are recounted as they took place. The village and wood were defended at various times by six German divisions, 11th, 240th, 20th, 214th and 21st Reserve as well as the 3rd Guards Division. It was 186 Brigade led by the determined **Brigadier General Roland Boys Bradford** that was the first British brigade to get close to the wood, managing to advance along the track to the west of

Brigadier Roland Boys Bradford.

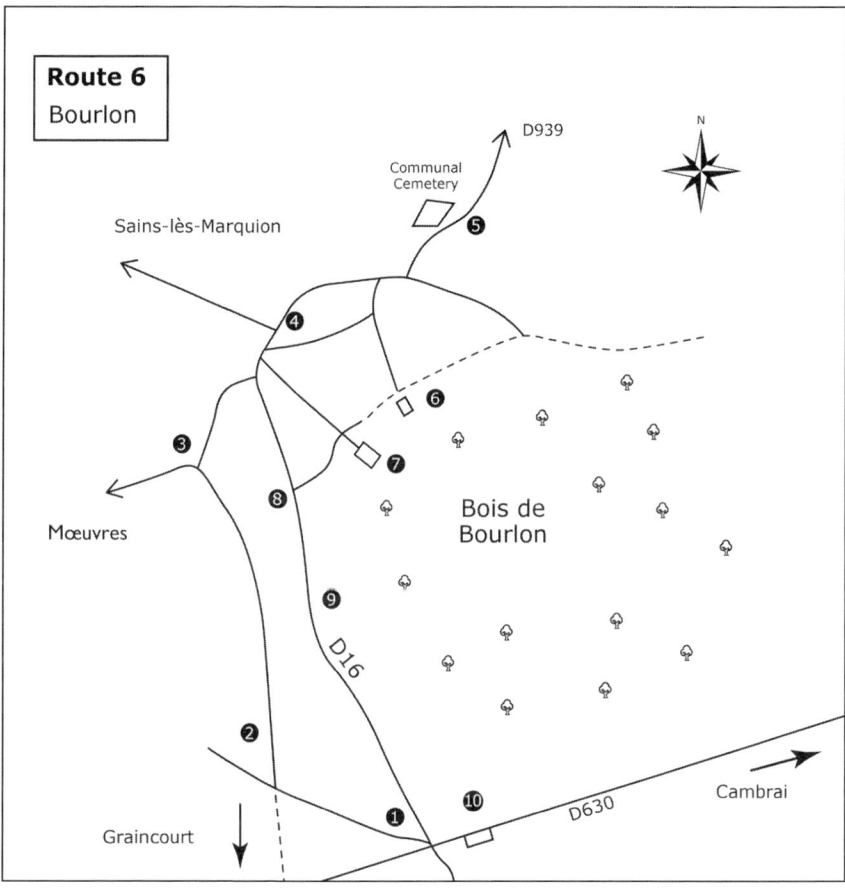

Bourlon on 21 November. One cannot help but think that, as the men of 186 Brigade moved north from Graincourt, there must have been a strong feeling that Bourlon would be taken that day. Certainly, had the men of 186 Brigade not been so tired and exhausted and had there been more men available Bourlon village would probably have been captured. But it was not to be, the tanks of G Battalion were late and even when the tanks did arrive they were unable to penetrate the German defences and were forced back by the weight of fire coming from Bourlon Wood. Though late in arriving, the tanks were not reluctant to press on and one or two even reached a point southwest of Bourlon village. Nevertheless, relieved by 185 Brigade, Bradford's 186 Brigade withdrew to Graincourt.

The main attack came on 23 November and the 40th Division reached the northern edge of Bourlon Wood and entered the village. Leading the attack along the track, west of the wood, was 121 Brigade with thirteen tanks from D Battalion going ahead of them. Organized into two composite companies, the left was commanded by **Major F. Cooper** and the right was under the command of **Major William Watson**, but of the thirteen tanks from D Battalion only seven reached the final objective. Nevertheless, despite the presence of tanks, the Germans regained their lost ground and by mid-afternoon troops were digging in. Watson, the author of *A Company of Tanks*, admits that he and the other tank commanders had not actually seen Bourlon Wood before or even met the troops of the 40th Division, writing that the wood dominated the whole countryside and beyond, 'Immediately in front of me on the hillside was the great dark mass of Bourlon Wood, square and impenetrable, covering the highest point of the hill and stretching over the skyline to the father slope, which we could not see.'

The next day orders were issued for the 40th Division to continue their advance and attack the village with the support of twelve tanks from I Battalion under the command of **Major Frank Vandervell**. On this occasion three companies of the 14/Highland Light Infantry (HLI) reached the station but were subsequently cut off. In attempting to reach the Highlanders on the next day the attack ran into problems and the Highlanders were overwhelmed. Their commander, **Lieutenant Colonel Clinton Battye**, was buried in the house where he died. The Germans, however, fought back tenaciously, *Unteroffizer* Hetschold of the Lehr Infantry Regiment (3rd Guards Division) recalling stopping a tank, probably from I Battalion:

> Suddenly from our left half rear came the clank of metal. A British tank was steering for us and was firing. Our comrades yelled and leapt for the sunken road. I heaved my gun round and loaded, there was no time for thought: the monster was within twenty metres of me. I fired at the place I had been taught. I could hear my gefreiter was also firing. There was a whirring noise and smoke appeared. Men jumped out of the monster and raced away. Driverless, it came past us burning.

During the night of 25 November the 40th Division was relieved by the 62nd Division, their objective being the northern sector of the wood and village as far as the railway. 186 Brigade took over the

Bourlon Wood positions from 119 Brigade and 187 Brigade relieved 121 Brigade. Major General John Ponsonby's 40th Division finally left the wood with horrific casualties of 172 officers and 3,191 other ranks killed, wounded or missing. In the whole of the campaign only the 29th Division suffered more and that was over a fourteen-day period. **Private Herbert Gregory** of 119 Company, Machine Gun Corps (MGC), had good reason to remember the hell of Bourlon Wood. Two limbers, containing badly wounded men, were hit by a shell close to where he was standing:

> When the limbers got to within thirty yards or so of the hospital, a tremendous shell came hurtling over and exploded, crash, right under the two limbers. The men and limbers were scattered in all directions, all being killed instantly. The mules lay dead in pools of their own blood, while the limbs of the unfortunate men were scattered about over the road: arms, legs and heads being severed as if with a scythe.

The plan of attack was for the 62nd Division and the Guards to attack eastwards, supported by twenty tanks from F and C Battalions, thereby capturing Bourlon and Fontaine and consolidating a line running along the northern slopes of Bourlon Ridge. **Major General Geoffrey Fielding**, commanding the Guards Division, was very much against the plan, which looked good on paper but was doomed from the outset. He was correct. The 62nd Division's brigades made little headway in the face of heavy fire whilst the 2/Guards Brigade battalions were back where they had started from by 1.00pm. Worse still, a group of tanks on the road leading up to Bourlon fell into an ambush just south of the chateau and no fewer than seven tanks were hit and put out of action. The Guards had not only lost a battle but had suffered 38 officers and 1,043 other ranks killed, wounded or missing. On 28 November the Germans began an intensive bombardment on Bourlon Wood just as the 47th Division was relieving the 62nd Division. Using a mixture of gas and high explosive, you can imagine the high number casualties sustained by both divisions. It was during this bombardment that 28-year-old **Private George Clare**, a stretcher bearer with the 5/Lancers, 3/Dismounted Cavalry Brigade, was part of the support allocated to the 40th Division. His fearless exposure to fire as he tended the wounded resulted in the award of the **Victoria Cross**. Sadly, he was killed by a shell a few hours afterwards and his body was lost. He is commemorated on the Cambrai Memorial, remembered at St Peter

George Clare VC (right) standing with an unidentified soldier.

Major Frederick Johnson VC.

and St Paul's Church, Cambridgeshire, and his name appears on the nearby Chatteris War Memorial. In the centre of the wood, another holder of the Victoria Cross, 27-year-old **Major Frederick Johnson**, commanding of 231/Field Company, was working with his company of sappers before his life was ended by a German sniper. His award of the coveted cross was made back in 1915, whilst he was a second lieutenant serving with 73/Field Company at Loos. Like George Clare, his body was also lost, and his name is commemorated on the Cambrai Memorial.

The German counterattack on 30 November saw two brigades of the 47th Division in the wood holding their own against the attack by *Generalleutnant* Otto von Moser's 3rd Guards Division. On the left of the wood the 2nd Division, commanded by **Major General Cecil Pereira**, was forming a defensive line north of the D930 on the night

Major General Cecil Pereira.

of 26–27 November. On the morning of the German counterattack German troops from the IR383, IR263 and IR50 together with IR80, IR87 and IR88 were seen massing for an attack in the area of **Quarry Wood**. Although the Germans were stopped on the left, some advances were made on the left near Lock 5 and the 1/Royal Berkshires temporarily lost three of their advanced posts, the slopes leading down to the Berkshires and Fusiliers' trenches soon becoming a killing ground as the British poured an accurate fire into the advancing Germans.

On 30 November **Captain Walter Stone** of the 17/Royal Fusiliers was in the centre of 99 Brigade's front and was holding the **Rat's Tail**, a long

Captain Walter Stone VC.

sap running at right angles to the front line. Stone, commanding A Company, quickly became isolated and by 10.30am the northern end of the Rat's Tail had been lost. Dispatching his company to safety, Stone remained with one platoon and its commander, **Lieutenant Soloman Benzecry**, and calmly stood of the parapet of the trench with a telephone sending back much valuable information regarding German troop movements. Stone was eventually killed with a shot to the head and his posthumous award of the **Victoria Cross** was gazetted in February 1918. Lieutenant Benzecry, in my opinion rather unfairly, only received a Mention in Dispatches. The bodies of both men were never recovered and their names are commemorated on the Cambrai Memorial. There is a memorial to Walter Stone in the Greenwich Cemetery, London. On 4 December the 47th Division, commanded by **Major General George Gorringe**, received orders to fall back to the Winter Line and withdrew to Graincourt. By the

Major General George Gorringe.

morning of 7 December the division was in position behind **Hughes Trench** and the Canal du Nord.

The route takes the track west of Bourlon Wood, where 186 Brigade first approached the wood and 99 Brigade made their stand on the Mœuvres road. From here a visit is made to the church on Rue de l'Église in Bourlon village and the former railway station where the 14/HLI were overwhelmed. We return using **Avenue du Bois** before a visit is made to the Canadian Memorial and the 1944 Memorial to the Maquisards. We return along the D16 to the junction with the D630.

Directions to start: The shrine at les Trois Cornets, which is almost opposite the D15 to Anneux, is best approached from the east at Cambrai or the west at Bapaume along the D930. In summer the shrine can be partially hidden by vegetation and **Route de Mœuvres** is a few metres past the turning to Bourlon. Parking is probably best in the layby on the right of the D930, just before the D15/16 to Bourlon.

Route description: Bourlon village was adopted by Hove, Brighton, after the war and I have focused attention on the actions of the 14/HLI in the village and those of 99 Brigade west of the wood. The actions in the wood itself are covered in the general description. From the shrine that marks the beginning of **Route de Mœuvres** ❶ continue past the farm buildings on the left towards the junction of tracks some 550m ahead. The bulk of 186 Brigade most probably used this track on their way up to Bourlon Wood on 21 November. The 40th Division had been forced marched from Lucheux arriving in Lebucquière on 22 November and, as if to compound the handicap, a meeting between **Lieutenant General Charles Woollcombe** and **Major General William Ponsonby**, the divisional commander, at Havrincourt postponed the 121 Brigade attack on Bourlon, as the number of tanks was considered insufficient. This may have had something to do with the German counterattack on 119 Brigade, but in any case orders were only received by the supporting artillery and failed to reach 121 Brigade until it was too late. The tragedy was now unfolding.

As you proceed along the track look to your left, you should see a small copse and quarry. This is where **Lieutenant Colonel Hugh Warden's** East Surreys (120 Brigade) waited for the orders to advance on Bourlon on 24–25 November and where two platoons of D Company, **1/Royal Berkshires**, under **Second Lieutenant Leach**, waited on 30 November. Stop at the junction of tracks.

At 9.30am on 23 November the 14/HLI, under the command of **Lieutenant Colonel Clinton Battye**, moved from Graincourt under orders of 121 Brigade, their orders being to take Bourlon village along with the 12/Suffolks led by 38-year-old **Lieutenant Colonel Theodore Eardley-Wilmot**. Battye had only been in command of the HLI since the beginning of July 1917 and from all accounts took the most direct route from Graincourt, advancing past the copse and quarry to the junction of tracks where you are now standing. It must have been at the junction, or close to it, that the HLI were subjected to a particularly accurate enemy artillery barrage that effectively killed or wounded all the men of 7 Platoon with the exception of the platoon commander. The 12/Suffolks advanced behind and to the left of the HLI, coming under heavy fire from the German trenches and the houses in the village.

Lieutenant Colonel Theodore Eardley-Wilmot.

Now cast you mind forward to 30 November when this was the 99 Brigade battlefield. You will remember that there were two brigades of the 47th Division in the wood whilst the 2nd Division was forming a defensive line north of the D930 to the west of the wood. The line defended by the 1/Berkshires (99 Brigade) ran from the ruins of the sugar factory on the D930, where the 1/Berkshire Battalion Headquarters was on 30 November, to a point some 750m west of Bourlon Wood.

Continue along the track for another 550m ❷ and stop. In front of you, running across the track from left to right, was the approximate position of the Berkshire B Company section posts, commanded by **Captain Donald Valentine**. B Company was positioned in eight section posts with the right flank in touch with the 6/London Rifles and the left in the sunken road leading towards the present-day motorway. On the morning of 30 November German troops from the IR383, IR263 and IR50 together with IR80, IR87 and IR88 were massing for an attack in the area of **Quarry Wood** (to the north) and after two days of shelling and constant sniping, a massive enemy attack was launched at first light. Several minutes later the first wave of enemy infantry appeared over the brow of the hill. Captain Valentine was in the sunken road:

> I was sitting, very sleepy, on the side of the road drinking cocoa when the nearest sentry came tumbling down from his post exclaiming with great eagerness: 'The SOS has gone up in twenty-seven different places and the Boche are coming over the 'ill in thousands.' Our artillery response to the SOS was immediate, and one of the quickest pieces of work I had seen ... Shelling was very heavy, but fortunately, as we had no set line of trenches, most of it was behind us, though a good deal fell nearer.

The first wave crumpled and died, giving the men time before the next attack at 11.25am. Once again the defeated German infantry retired over the hill before a third wave attacked at 2.30pm. This time it came from the direction of Bourlon Wood and the two reserve platoons from D Company, which had been waiting in the copse behind B Company, were brought up as reinforcements. A desperate, and at times hand-to-hand, battle was fought for an hour and was finally resolved when the 6/Londons brought up three machine guns. Incredibly, the Germans massed for a further assault at 4.10pm against the left flank but this was halted by the 2nd Division Artillery. *Oberstleutnant* Breitenbach, RIR80, was the commander of the forward troops during the attack and was witness to the German assault:

> Initially there was artillery fire on the enemy positions, two hours [sic] later our infantry began to attack. Because my regiment was to follow in the second wave, I was able to observe the advance of the others in peace. Heavy artillery fire was coming down on the lines of infantry to my left. Gradually there was a change in behaviour. In contrast to the previous momentum, hesitation and reluctance occurred. On one occasion there was a move to the rear. This was an unsatisfactory sight which made the blood in my veins run cold.

B Company casualties were 46 killed and wounded and, according to **Major General Pereira**, they claimed to have killed at least 500 of the enemy. The battalion finally withdrew to Hermies on the night of 3 December.

We are now moving north, away from the 99 Brigade battle, and back to Bourlon village and the last stand of Lieutenant Colonel

Battye's HLI. Continue along the track until you meet the junction where there is a wooden shrine ❸. A German machine-gun position was here before it was overrun by the tanks on 24 November. This is probably the point where the HLI and the Suffolks proceeded across the fields, keeping to the edge of the wood to avoid the German machine-gun fire. The HLI war diary is understandably sparse and does not mention the tanks joining them, but it is known that twelve tanks from I Battalion entered the village at 3.30pm closely followed by the HLI and Suffolks. As the tanks reached the village there was no sign of the infantry as they were held up by machine-gun fire from the surrounding houses. Battye established Battalion Headquarters in a farmhouse somewhere close to **Rue Victor Lacroix** whilst the remaining two companies continued towards the railway station where they were to await the appearance of the cavalry. The war diary tells us that one company became lost and eventually turned up at Battalion Headquarters and was kept in reserve.

Our route turns right at the shrine and follows **Rue de Mœuvres** for 400m to the junction with the D16 (Rue Victor Lacroix). At the junction, turn left towards the church ❹. The layout of the village has changed very little since 1917 and the church, now restored, contains

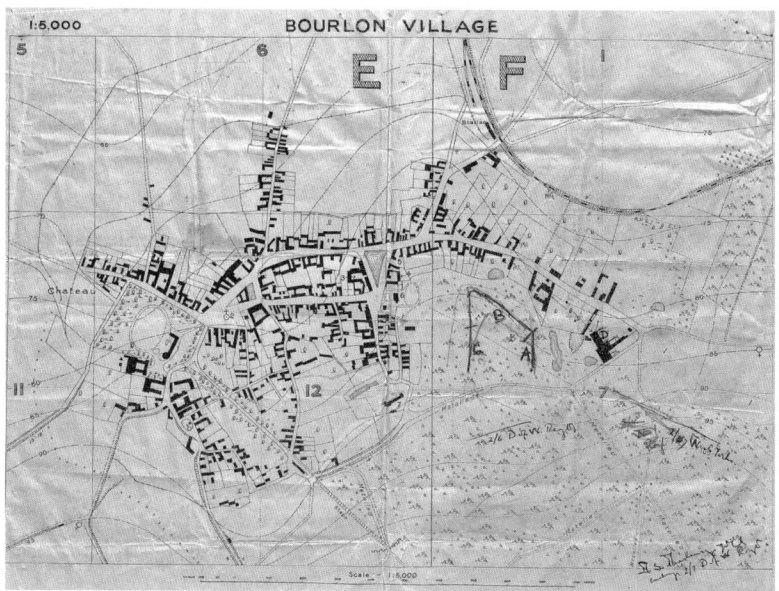

A map of Bourlon village and part of the wood that belonged to Second Lieutenant Harry Hartley, 2/7 Duke of Wellingtons. Hartley was wounded on 27 November.

The church and war memorial at Bourlon.

a wooden plaque on the left-hand side of the nave presented to the village by the Tank Corps. In 1928, the high altar was dedicated to the memory of the 40th Division by the surviving men who fought here in 1917. Outside the church is a memorial to **Lieutenant Graham Lyall**, who was awarded the **Victoria Cross** in September 1918. Meanwhile the tanks, now devoid of their supporting infantry, sustained heavy losses. **Second Lieutenant George Parsons**, commanding I.28 *Incomparable*, recalled moving up a narrow road to the Bourlon Crest: 'There were eight tanks in Indian file – I was fifth and remember seeing Major Vandervell and Captain Keane literally staggering back down the road, white as sheets. I heard afterwards that with Captain Monaghan they were near the crest, when a shell took Monaghan's head right off.' Parsons felt they should not have left a group of tanks without an officer and with no one in command the tanks came to a halt. This may have accounted for the demise of a further eight of the tanks, five of whom had broken down, two were hit by enemy fire and one, I.28, fell into a deep ditch and was abandoned. Owing to the lateness of the day and when the infantry did not appear, the remaining four tanks withdrew, leaving the 14/HLI and the 12/Suffolks in the village, with Battalion Headquarters of the Suffolks in the quarry north of the chateau.

Abandoned tanks of F and G Battalions in Bourlon wood.

In the meantime three companies of the HLI moved to the north of the village to await the arrival of the cavalry, experiencing few casualties en route for the railway station whilst the Suffolks came under attack almost as soon as they began to advance. A strong local counterattack by the Lehr Battalion drove them back. It is unlikely that the Suffolks got as far as the church before retiring to the west of the wood. In the meantime, in the ever-increasing darkness the companies of the HLI had occupied the railway station, not fully realizing they were now isolated and surrounded. **Reserve Leutnant Schafrinna**, serving with the Fusilier Guard Regiment, arrived at the station only to come under heavy fire from the British. He decided to wait until the following morning before assaulting the British position:

> I orientated myself over the exact situation, the layout and strength of the British nest of resistance. Then I issued the following orders: one assault troop under *Vizefeldwebel* Maushake, together with one heavy machine gun commanded by *Vizefeldwebel* Schade, was to capture the loading ramp. 2nd Platoon, commanded by *Vizefeldwebel* van Hoorn, was to provide fire support from a flank to aid the advance of the assault troop and was to engage any of the enemy attempting to escape.

Despite the fact that there was obstinate defence, the assault succeeded, thanks to the total commitment of the assault troop. The enemy, attempting to withdraw, ran straight into a curtain of machine gun fire. The nest of resistance had been garrisoned by approximately 150 men and fifteen machine guns.

In the British lines preparation were being made on 25 November to join up with the HLI but there was only one fresh battalion available, the 13/East Surreys. Unbeknown to them their advance would be without the support of tanks or artillery. **Lieutenant Colonel Warden** was ordered to clear the western side of the village and had already met Battye at his headquarters in Bourlon village during the hours of darkness on 24 November and now sent word back to the battalion to meet him in the copse and quarry close to the D630 at 3.30am. The East Surreys must have followed the route of the HLI into the village and whilst Warden headed for Battye's headquarters, the battalion headed along the main street, past the church. **Corporal Fred Wynne** remembered the street was quite wide with small houses on each side and their orders were to mop up the village and relieve the men of HLI. Wynne had almost reached the centre of the village when the defending Germans opened fire:

> We were sitting ducks. It was impossible to be certain where the machine guns were, but without doubt the bullets came from the upper windows of the houses somewhere near the crossroads. We fired into every window we could aim at. The machine guns then stopped. Of course we thought, or hoped, that the hundreds of bullets we had fired into the windows had effectively destroyed the machine gun nests.

Wynne and the East Surreys were near to the church at the crossroads on the main street and they were still unaware that the HLI in the station had been overwhelmed by *Leutnant* Schafrinna and his company. Back at Battye's headquarters German infantry were attacking the house which was repelled by the reserve company of HLI and some of the East Surreys. At 7.15am Battye left the building and, on crossing a road to visit a Lewis gun position, was hit by a burst of fire. Staggering back, he had enough time to tell Warden he had been hit before he died. The Adjutant, **Captain Gilbert Manford**, assumed temporary command of the battalion. Battye was initially buried in the garden of the building and then reinterred at Mœuvres Communal Cemetery Extension. The East Surreys in the main street

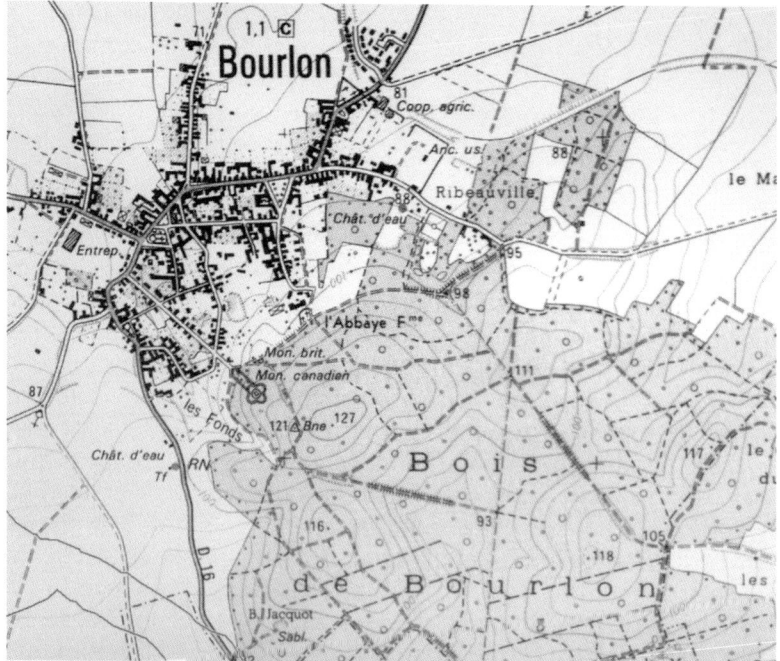

A modern map showing the communal cemetery and former railway station, the church, Bourlon Wood Cemetery and the Canadian Memorial.

made little further progress and were eventually reunited with Warden at Battalion Headquarters in the southwest of the village. The battalion, what was left of them and including Fred Wynne, would not leave Bourlon until midday on 27 November.

Continue along the main street, past the church and Mairie to where there is another fork in the road – Rue de la Gare. Bear left along here towards the communal cemetery and in 300m you will arrive at the former station buildings opposite the cemetery ❺. Sadly, the station has been demolished but the former buildings are now contained in the open ground on the right of the road and the railway trackbed can still be seen amongst the ever-encroaching vegetation.

From the former railway station walk across to the communal cemetery where you will find at the far end two graves positioned side by side and marked '*inconnu*'. These are two of the resistance men shot by the Germans in 1944, and a memorial stone to eleven more is close to the Canadian Memorial. Leave the communal cemetery and retrace your steps to the fork in the road. Turn right

Bourlon Wood Cemetery.

here and then, after 70m, turn left. You now have a choice of routes. If you carry straight ahead, along **Rue de l'Abbaye**, look out for the CWGC signpost and you will come to **Bourlon Wood Cemetery** ❻, composed of entirely 1918 burials.

There are now almost 250 Canadians buried here and of these some 10 are unidentified. Having visited the cemetery, the track running behind the cemetery – **Chemin de Cambrai** – leads back towards the village and the Canadian Memorial, where you can rejoin the original route. However, be warned, this track can become muddy. In the Middle Ages this track, which joined Bourlon to Fontaine-Notre-Dame, was subject of a road-improvement scheme and tons of rubble was poured into the foundations, depressions were filled and deep ditches were dug to drain off the winter rain.

For those wishing to bypass **Bourlon Wood Cemetery**, turn right into **Grand Rue** which will take you back to the church. Turn left at the church into the main street and passing the crossroads where Corporal Wynne and his comrades fired into the upper windows of the houses, continue for 100m to **Avenue du Bois** which you will see on your left and leads straight down to the **Canadian Memorial** on the edge of the wood ❼. Although the memorial is dedicated to the Canadian Troops who took Bourlon in September 1918, it is still worthy of a visit. The monument is erected on ground donated by the Compte de Franqueville, who was Mayor of Bourlon in 1918, and

The Canadian Memorial.

is similar in type to that at Courcelette on the Somme and Crest Farm at Passchendaele, being composed of the standard block of white Quebec granite. Both these sites are described in earlier editions of this guidebook series.

Anneux British Cemetery.

Leave the memorial and turn left into **Rue du Marais**. After the road bends round to the right a pathway can be seen on the second bend taking you through to a cul de sac which, after some 60m, takes you to the D16 ❽. Turn left and continue downhill and just before the water tower on the right is a small turning leading to a television mast ❾. This is the site where the Canadian Memorial was originally intended to be erected. Return to the D16 and continue downhill, keeping Bourlon Wood on your left, to the junction with the D630 and your vehicle.

Private Bertie Hopkinson.

This is a good moment to visit **Anneux British Cemetery** which is a few metres from where you left your vehicle ❿. On entering the cemetery one of the first things that strikes the battlefield visitor is the staggering number of unidentified burials. Of the 1,013 burials, 459 men remain unidentified. It is only when you realize that this number represents just under 50 per cent you begin to understand the horrors of warfare. Amongst the identified there are ninety-six men who fought in the 1917 Cambrai campaign, the remainder served with the 57th, 63 (RND), 52nd and the 1st and 4th Canadian Divisions during the Second Battle of Cambrai in 1918. The original cemetery was made by the 57th Division Burial Officer and by various other units in October 1918. At the Armistice it contained 131 graves but was then greatly increased when graves were brought in from the surrounding battlefields and small cemeteries in the area, including the communal cemeteries at Graincourt and Anneux. There are two identified Tank Corps casualties from the B Battalion attack on Fontaine on 23 November, 23-year-old **Private Harold Marshall** (II.F.9) lies close to 20-year-old **Private Bertie Hopkinson** (II.F.21), and they were more than likely victims of the flak lorries employed by the Germans.

Route 7
Marcoing and Masnières

Three short tours beginning at: the railway station at Marcoing Victoria Cross action and ending at Masnières

Distances: Marcoing: 1.4km/1mile, the Arthur Lascelles Victoria Cross action: 0.4km/0.2 miles, Masnières: 2.9km/1.8 miles
Grade: Easy
Suitable for: ⛶ 🚲 🚗
Map: Cambrai-Bertincourt 2507 SB

General description and context: This is a route that combines a short walk/ride at Marcoing with a journey by vehicle to **Marcoing British Cemetery** and the lock at **Bracheux** before continuing to Masnières for another walk/ride. Five Victoria Crosses were awarded at Marcoing and Masnières and the sites of four of these actions are looked at in detail. The route concludes with a short drive up the main street of Masnières (D644) to the Newfoundland Caribou. The energetic amongst us should be reminded that it is possible to ride or walk from Marcoing to Masnières using the D15 and returning via the towpath on the south side of the canal.

Marcoing played a strategic role in the functioning of the Hindenburg Line and thus it was vital to overcome any opposition in **Nine Wood**, 1km to the north of Marcoing, particularly as it commanded the valley of Noyelles (see **Route 10**) on the canal below it. On 20 November tanks from H Battalion advanced on Nine Wood, Bois des Neufs on French IGN maps, along with 86 Brigade. Thus the 1/Royal Guernsey Light Infantry, 86 Brigade, found itself in action for the first time in its history in assisting the clearance of the northwest corner of the wood. **Private Stanley Blicq**, the author of *Norman Ten Hundred*, was with the Guernsey's (1/RGLI) as they charged up the long incline to the wood: 'They went for it hell for leather in a long line of skirmishers. Their rifles cracked with the rapidity that tells the marksman – and they could shoot! But Fritz would not have any. They did not like the nasty gleam of those Norman bayonets.' With the wood taken, the Guernseys, who referred to themselves as the

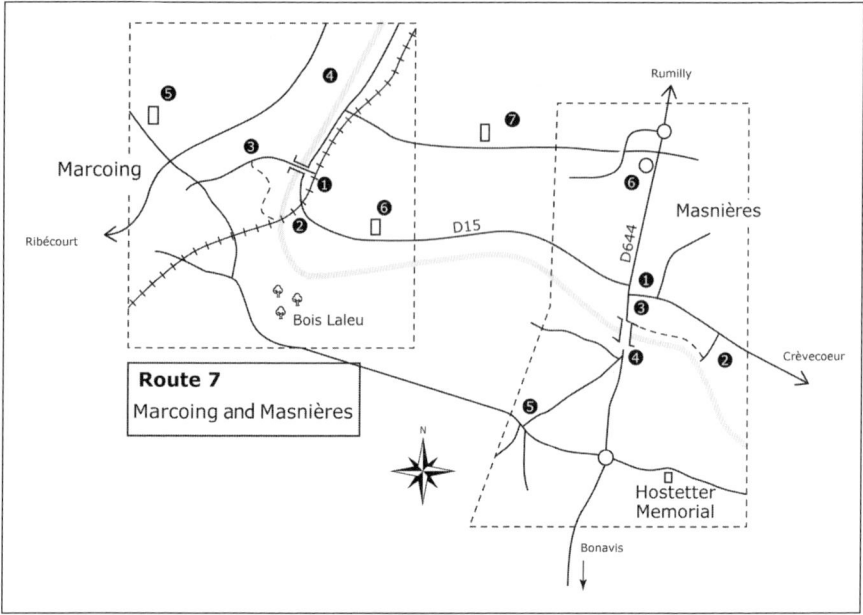

Normans, were on the left flank of 86 Brigade and held off German attacks coming from the north. After securing the trenches from the bend southeast of Noyelles to Nine Wood the brigade was relieved by the 6th Division after dark on 21 November and went into billets in Marcoing.

Shielded by the support line and connected by rail and canal to Cambrai, Marcoing was used for the stationing of German troops and was captured on 20 November by the 6th Division. Eight tanks from A Battalion reached the canal at 10.50am and prevented the German Pioneer Company 108 from destroying the railway bridge. Fourteen more tanks from B Battalion arrived to the west of the village at 11.30am and took up position on the railway embankment firing on snipers. However, in the absence of supporting infantry Marcoing could not be cleared of enemy troops entirely and it was left to troops of 71 Brigade to begin the difficult task of house clearance. **87 Brigade** arrived in Marcoing via Couillet Wood at approximately midday, halting just short of Marcoing to allow the 1/KOSB to clear the opposition and establish two crossings over the canal. The **1/Border Regiment** arrived in Marcoing at 12.00pm and two companies crossed the railway bridge with a third crossing over the lock, securing the railway station, the scene of the Borderer's second **Victoria Cross** of the war.

At Marcoing Copse (Bois Laleu on IGN maps), 37-year-old **Lieutenant Colonel John Sherwood-Kelly**, commanding the 1/Royal Inniskilling Fusiliers (RIF), was pinned down, along with B Company of the 1/Borderers, by enemy machine-gun fire from the buildings on the far bank. Having brought up a tank, the opposition was overcome and the battalion crossed via the lock at Bracheux led by Sherwood-Kelly. Advancing up the high ground to the north of Marcoing, the 1/Borderers, who had come up on the left of Sherwood-Kelly, and the 1/RIF unsuccessfully attacked the enemy positions along the Masnières–Beaurevoir Line. Darkness and heavy defensive fire prompted the British to dig in. Sherwood-Kelly was awarded the **Victoria Cross** for his part in the day's actions. He was commissioned in November 1914 and posted with 1/KOSB to Gallipoli where he was awarded the DSO at Chocolate Hill. He became the commanding officer of the 1/RIF in April 1917 and died in London in 1931. He is buried at Brookwood Cemetery.

Lieutenant Colonel John Sherwood-Kelly VC, commander of the 1/Royal Inniskilling Fusiliers.

Flying Fox II *lying in the canal, having collapsed the bridge on Rue du Lain.*

Masnières was a strategic strongpoint that protected several crossings over the canal that needed to be captured to give the British cavalry a crossing en route to their objective and was completely destroyed. Shortly before noon thirteen tanks of F Battalion, under the command of **Major Phillip Hammond**, arrived in Masnières. Two tanks suffered mechanical problems and F.22 *Flying Fox II*, in trying to cross the main bridge on Rue Lain, completely destroyed the superstructure and fell into the canal, severely hampering the advance of the cavalry. The image of the tank lying in the canal is one of the most famous from the battle and the collapse of the bridge at Masnières demonstrated a fundamental flaw in the plan, often ignored by many accounts. This flaw, which the failure to cross the Canal de Saint-Quentin placed on further options for tanks and cavalry on the right flank, forced Haig to switch attention to Bourlon and the left flank. It was the beginning of the end. Le Rue Vertes was taken by the 11/Rifle Brigade (20th Division) and one tank forcing the defending Germans to withdraw across the main bridge over the canal on Rue Lain. Shortly before the collapse of the bridge, troops of the 4/Worcester (88 Brigade) had managed to get two companies across the canal but were stopped by heavy machine-gun fire.

At 11.40 on 20 November the Canadian Cavalry Brigade was ordered to advance on Masnières, despite the fact that the situation between Masnières and Marcoing was still unclear and erroneous reports were circulating that 88 Brigade had captured all of its objectives. Sensing an opportunity for a cavalry breakout, **Brigadier General John Seeley**, commanding the brigade, ordered the Fort Garry Horse across the canal. Certainly, by this time the bridge on Rue Lain had been destroyed by *Flying Fox II*, forcing the Fort Garry Horse to use the lock southeast of Masnières. Eventually only B Squadron crossed the canal and galloped toward the ridge east of Rumilly. In the meantime, it was decided that the lock was unsuitable for a large number of horses to pass across and two riders were sent to recall B Squadron but were unfortunately unable to halt them. B Squadron soon came under

Brigadier General John Seeley, commander of the Canadian Cavalry Brigade.

heavy fire and **Captain Duncan Campbell** was killed leaving 33-year-old **Lieutenant Harcus Strachan** to continue the advance. Ordering the squadron to charge a gun battery, they suffered heavy casualties before retiring into a sunken road east of Rumilly. **Gefreiter Albert Müller**, serving with ID 49, remembered being pushed into the line by an artillery officer after an arduous forced march: 'We took up positions in a sunken road and received the advancing British cavalry with murderous small arms fire. The attack withered away, we took many prisoners. Dead horses, men and fine leather equipment lay around in tangled heaps. We also seized numerous riderless horses. Our casualties were slight.'

Lieutenant Harcus Strachan VC, who brought the survivors of the Fort Garry Horse back from Rumilly.

Eventually 68 out of 127 men returned on foot to British lines. In addition to Strachan's **Victoria Cross** the squadron was awarded three MCs, two Distinguished Conduct Medals (DCM) and four Military Medals (MM). Campbell is buried at Flesquières Hill British Cemetery. Commissioned in September 1916, Strachan was awarded the MC in May 1917 and was wounded a matter of weeks later and died in Vancouver in May 1982.

Although the British got into Rumilly, the defenders of the Masnières–Beaurevoir Line proved too strong and the offensive was stopped at Masnières, which remained the northeastern limit of the English advance. The Newfoundland Caribou marks the line reached by the 1/Newfoundland Regiment. On 25 January 1918, His Majesty King George V conferred the title of 'Royal' on the regiment in recognition of its service, a distinction that was awarded to no other regiment of the British Army whilst fighting was still in progress.

By the end of 20 November, 88 Brigade had fought their way into the outskirts of Masnières and overnight mopping-up parties moved through Masnières, clearing out all resistance except for in the north of the town and a small party still in the catacombs at its centre. The following day the last defenders and consolidated hold on the town was cleared and according to the 86 Brigade War diary, by 23 November the whole brigade had crossed the canal and occupied the trenches to the north of Masnières.

Directions to start: The former Marcoing railway station is on the east side of Marcoing near to the Canal de Saint-Quentin. It can be reached via the D29 from Ribécourt-la-Tour, on the D15 from Masnières or from Cambrai via Noyelles-sur-Escaut. Once in Marcoing follow Rue de la Gare over the canal, turning right into Place de la Gare. Park here ❶.

Route description: For the sake of clarity the actions at Marcoing will concentrate on 20 November whilst those of **Captain Arthur Lascelles** and the 14/DLI will be confined to 3 December. At Masnières the focus will be on the German counterattack of 30 December.

There is still some controversy surrounding the crossing and capture of the railway bridge at Marcoing. According to the *Official History* the German pioneer regiment attached to ID54 mined the bridge and the detonator cables were cut by **Second Lieutenant John Bailey**, a reconnaissance officer with A Battalion. We are also told that **Lieutenant Arthur Dalby**, commanding B.23 *Bandit II*, took his tank along the railway embankment and found a party of Germans running out a cable to detonate the bridge and, after a short action, a party of Royal Engineers under the command of **Major Basil Watson** arrived and Dalby assisted them in making the bridge safe. This may of course have occurred later during a second attempt to blow the bridge. Whatever the case, the bridge was saved from destruction.

The old railway bridge, Marcoing.

Lieutenant Colonel Archibald Ellis, who crossed the railway bridge at 12.20pm with two companies of the 1/Border Regiment.

Sergeant Charles Spackman VC, who won his cross at the former Marcoing railway station.

Marcoing railway station, which has now fallen into disuse.

Second Lieutenant Edward Leigh-Jones, commanding B.9 *Black Bess*, was probably on the far side of the railway bridge: 'We were on our objectives at 12.00, fuelled up, with ammunition oil and grease, which was brought along by tanks on sledges. Then we sat down to await further orders and above all to wait for the promised huge reinforcement of infantry and cavalry.'

At 12.20pm two companies of the 1/Border Regiment, under the command of **Lieutenant Colonel Archibald Ellis**, crossed the railway bridge whilst C Company, led by **Second Lieutenant William Denareaz**, crossed at the nearby lock. It was at the former railway station that 26-year-old **Sergeant Charles Spackman** attacked a machine gun positioned in the centre of the railway track. Realizing that it would be impossible for the troops to advance, he continued through heavy fire to the gun which was 180m away. Despite there being no cover, Spackman hit the gunner with his first shot and then shot the second gunner. He finally rushed the position and, after bayoneting the third man, captured the gun. Spackman had previously served in Gallipoli in 1915 with the 29th Division and on demobilization worked as a bank messenger. He survived the war and died in May 1969.

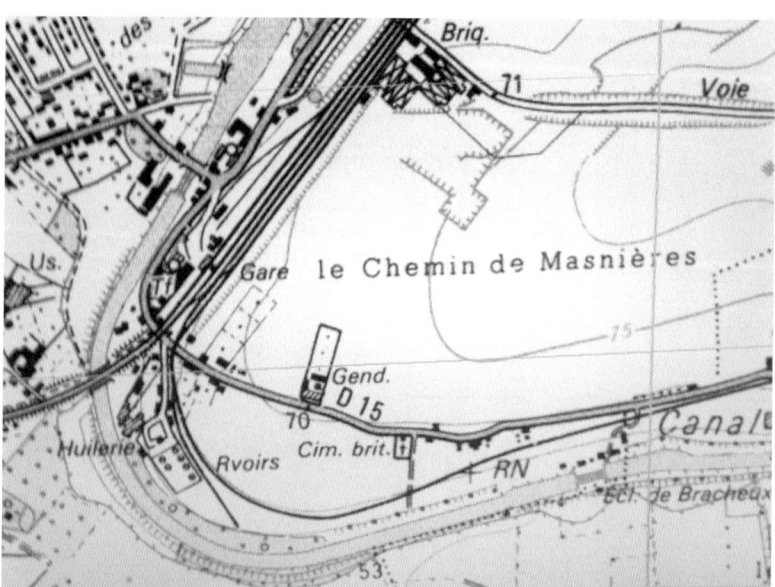

A modern-day map showing the old railway bridge, the railway yard and the site of Captain Arthur Lascelles' Victoria Cross action.

To get to the disused railway bridge ❷ leave the station and cross the canal via the road bridge, turning left to reach the towpath. With the canal on your left, walk or ride to where the former railway bridge crosses over the canal. You can either walk back the way you came or continue along the footpath that eventually has its junction with the D15 ❸. Turn right onto Rue de la Gare which will take you back to the road bridge in 200m.

The two tanks from A Battalion may have been those that got closest to Cambrai on 20 November, commanded by **Second Lieutenant Cyril Charles**, in A.52 *Artful Alice II*, and **Lieutenant John Lipscombe**, in A.55 *Aggressive II*. They had been taken across the canal by **Captain David Raikes**, a section commander with 3 Company, A Battalion, and were sent forward to 87 Brigade at the former railway station. Once there Raikes was handed a message:

> On receipt of a message from the infantry, stating there were still machine guns firing from the Talma Château, I ordered these two officers (Charles and Lipscombe) to fire into the rear of it as they went by, and also arranged for two platoons of infantry to move up the left side of the canal to clear out the chateau.

Talma Chateau was almost certainly occupied at the time by the headquarters of IR387 and was soon to become the temporary home

Talma Chateau today.

of 86 Brigade. The advance to the north by the 1/Borderers continued with A and D Companies to the east of the railway line and C Company to the west and it was probably C Company that cleared the machine guns from **Talma Chateau** ❹. A Company met heavy fire as they advanced on the ammunition pits on the lower slopes of the Rumilly Spur. At 1.30pm, after making contact with Lieutenant Colonel John Sherwood-Kelly's battalion, plans were made for a combined attack. However, the attack was cancelled as the 1/RIF was unable to advance in the face of heavy fire, and unfortunately the message did not get through to **Captain Johnson** and C Company on the far side of the canal and they attacked southwest of **Flot Farm** with one tank from A Battalion – probably A.52 *Artful Alice II*. Lipscombe's A.55 *Aggressive II* had previously been hit and Lipscombe wounded. The attack was successful resulting in the capture of nineteen prisoners and two machine guns, but this meant that their positions were now effectively open to flanking attacks, particularly from the right. C Company was subsequently ordered back to its original line before an enemy flank could be fully organized. As the proposed attack was still on hold, the line was consolidated during the evening of 20–21 November. The 1/Borderers were relieved late on 25 November and moved back to Marcoing and took temporary shelter in cellars. Marcoing was almost completely undamaged and showed very

Marcoing Communal Cemetery.

little sign that any hostilities had occurred there or nearby. A cache of German weapons, clothing and rations found close by came as a welcome surprise to the men. They remained here for two days before they were ordered to move out to their former section of the line. Battalion headquarters were located in the railway station.

This is probably a good moment to drive to **Marcoing Communal Cemetery** ❺ which is in the northwestern corner of the village. From the centre of the village head towards the church, following the D29 towards Ribécourt-la-Tour, just before leaving Marcoing turn into the Rue de l'Égalité and the cemetery entrance is at the end of the road. The war graves are located within two plots in the centre of this relatively small cemetery.

The cemetery was used by the Germans in 1917 and 129 of their men were removed in 1919 and 8 British POWs who were buried here by the Germans were later reinterred at St Souplet British Cemetery, near Le Cateau. There are now nearly twenty First World War casualties and a small number of casualties from the Second World War. **Second Lieutenant Robert Sparks** was only 19 years old when he was killed on 22 November 1917 serving with the 2/Royal Fusiliers. His name is also commemorated by a marble plaque in Holy Trinity Church, Richmond. **Private William Fletcher** of the Royal Army Medical Corps was killed by an exploding shell on 26 November 1917 whilst on stretcher-bearing duties. **Private James**

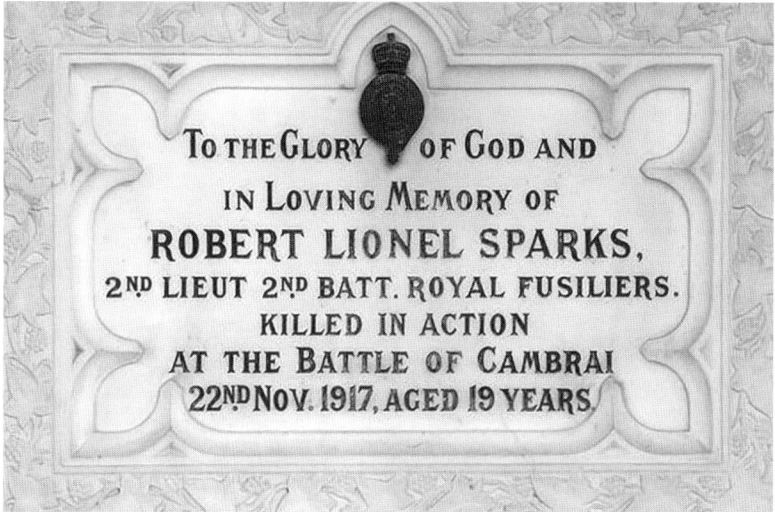

Memorial to Second Lieutenant Robert Sparks, Holy Trinity Church, Richmond.

Burns was another 19-year-old who was killed on 30 November. He was serving with the 4/Worcesters and was the son of James and Mary Burns. Finally, if you are looking for a headstone on which to place your cross of remembrance, look no further than **Private John Leahy** of the 14/Durham Light Infantry who was killed on 25 November 1917. He is also remembered on the Salisbury Memorial in Guildhall Square, Salisbury. The single 1940 casualty, who died on 11 May, was 22-year-old **Lance Corporal David Clarke**, 1/Royal Scots. His battalion was at Wavre, south of Louvain, in May 1940 but Clarke most probably died in Marcoing.

Leave the cemetery and rejoin the D15 just below the railway station and, keeping the canal and the lock on the right, follow the road round a left-hand bend before crossing the old railway line. From here it is some 500m along the D15 to **Marcoing British Cemetery** ❻, which you will see on the left side of the road. There is plenty of parking outside the entrance. I suggest you enter the cemetery after visiting the site of Captain Arthur Lascelles' Victoria Cross action. You may of course wish to drive to Marcoing British Cemetery, in which case from the railway yard continue along the D15, past the police station and park outside the cemetery. The Lascelles' Victoria Cross site is about 270m from the cemetery towards Masnières and can be reached by walking along the former railway line.

During the night of 3 December, the final day of the German counterattack, 87 Brigade was relieved by the 16 Brigade

Marcoing British Cemetery.

(6th Division) which was subjected to an attack at first light by the Germans intent on removing them from the canal loop north of Marcoing. The 14/DLI, with three companies forward, was on the right of the British line with its right flank on the canal and the 1/King's Shropshire Light Infantry (KSLI) was on the left. Whilst the Durham's left and centre companies were reasonably well protected by trenches, A Company was in a shallow ditch which offered little if any protection. A Company, under **Captain Arthur Lascelles**, was driven out of its ditch at 10.30am and Lascelles was wounded but refused to receive treatment. Jumping up onto the parapet, he and the twelve survivors rushed the enemy and succeeded in pushing them back. A third attack was launched at 12.15pm against the whole frontage of the DLI and KSLI and during the confusion Lascelles escaped. Lascelles received two more wounds but his leadership and daring during the attack was recognized with the award of the Victoria Cross. The Germans' superiority in numbers eventually overpowered the two battalions and the British were forced back to an outpost line east of Marcoing. Lascelles was killed on 7 November 1918, just four days before the Armistice, and is buried in Dourlers Communal Cemetery.

Captain Arthur Lascelles VC.

Retrace your steps to **Marcoing British Cemetery** and your vehicle. The cemetery was formed after the Armistice by the concentration of casualties from 1917 and 1918 from local battlefields and from those in Rumilly German Cemetery. There are now almost 400 casualties of the First World War commemorated here of which over half are unidentified. This is a cemetery shared with the men and boys of 1918 and of the 181 identified casualties, 77 are the results of actions in November and December 1917. The twenty-four special memorials can be found behind the Cross of Sacrifice. There are seven identified casualties of the 3 December German attack on the 1/KSLI and 14/DLI. **Second Lieutenant George Blake**, aged 30 (II.C.13), was killed on 3 December serving with the 1/KSLI, receiving his commission in December 1916 and joining the battalion in February 1917. He was educated at Clifton College in Bristol and then studied law before enlisting as a private in the Inns of Court Officer Training

Corps. He is also commemorated at St Oswald's Church, Oswestry, at Clifton School and on Trowbridge War Memorial. Two other members of the battalion, **Privates Leonard Downing** (II.C.19) and **Arthur Leay** (II.C.11), both died of wounds on 4 December. **Private John Riddell** (Sp. Mem. 21), serving with the 14/DLI, was killed on 3 December. He came from a farming family at Elsdon in Northumberland where his name appears on the church war memorial. Seven identified men of the Fort Garry Horse, all killed on 20 November, are also buried here and were probably originally buried at Rumilly German Cemetery. **Private Kenneth MacDonald**, aged 22 (Sp. Mem. 18), was originally from Aldersyde in Alberta and was awarded the MM in May 1917. Another MM winner was 24-year-old **Lance Corporal Otto Dunning** (Sp. Mem. 9), who was awarded the medal in July 1917. He came from Prince Edward Island and his brother, 19-year-old Claud Dunning, was killed in 1916 serving with the 600th Battalion CEF. **Private Arthur Jensen**, aged 21 (II.C.1), was a member of B Squadron when he was killed and came from Aetna in Alberta. Both Arthur and his older brother James enlisted in the army, Arthur joining the 13/Canadian Mounted Rifles in 1915 and when it was broken up transferring to B Squadron, Fort Garry Horse. James survived the war. All seven men are commemorated on the Fort Garry Horse Memorial Wall in Winnipeg, which was dedicated on 12 November 1995 in honour of all the members of the Fort Garry Horse who have died on active service with the regiment since its formation in 1912. Of the 1918 casualties the oldest man here is 51-year-old **Major Edward Sherson** (I.E.23) of the

Second Lieutenant George Blake.

Lance Corporal Otto Dunning.

2/Auckland Regiment who was killed at Crèvecoeur on 30 September 1918. He is one of forty New Zealanders who died in the attempt to take the bridge. **Second Lieutenant Frederick Weale**, aged 19 (II.E.20/21), was shot down in flames in his 57 Squadron DH.4 whilst in aerial combat with German fighters on 2 October 1918. His observer, 22-year-old **Second Lieutenant Ellis Preece** (II.E.20/21), was also killed. As you leave the cemetery look to the north across the D15 towards the Masnières–Beaurevoir Line to see the ground over which John Sherwood-Kelly led his Inniskillings on 20 November.

L'Église Saint-Martin, Masnières.

Leave the cemetery in your vehicle and turn right towards Masnières, continuing along the D15. As the outskirts of Masnières are approached you will come to some large silos on the right, some 400m before a roundabout. Go straight across the roundabout on Rue de Marcoing and continue for another 200m where there is a fork in the road. Take the left fork to reach the junction with the D644, turn left and then first right to find the church straight ahead of you. Park here ❶.

The original l'Église Saint-Martin was destroyed in 1917 and the replacement building was set back by 6m. The new l'Église Saint-Martin was inaugurated in 1933 and is one of the five churches restored by Pierre Leprince-Ringuet. Marcel Gaumont created several sculptural works in the church including the pediment depicting St Martin handing his cloak to a beggar. The facade of the church is decorated with several concrete reliefs. Completely destroyed, the village was classified in the red zone in 1919 and was only rebuilt through a large philanthropic gift by **Madame Burchard-Hostetter**, the mother of the 20-year-old American pilot **Theodore Hostetter** who was killed in 1918 over Masnières whilst flying a Sopwith Camel with No. 3 Squadron.

Masnières is honeycombed with catacombs which have many exits in the village and those in which the 1/RGLI waited before the battle on 30 November, were part of a huge complex located directly under the Cambrai–Saint-Quentin Road, where the present D15 crosses over it to the east and the west in the direction of Crèvecoeur and Marcoing. The Germans were eventually evicted from the catacombs on 21 November.

Although a German counterattack was expected on 30 November, very few imagined an attack from the south. At 7.00pm the whole front of 86 Brigade was shelled. Stanley Blicq was at 86 Brigade Headquarters when the first shells landed:

A modern-day map of Masnières showing the Newfoundland Caribou and the area south of the canal.

> A shell, heavy, unmistakably from a huge howitzer, crashed with a mighty uproar into a small house and demolished it at a stroke. Then another and another, and still another, what was he searching for? From the doorway of Brigade Headquarters I looked into the night and listened to the whistle of shells passing overhead into our lines.

The 29th Division's front was held by 86 and 87 Brigades. The 86 Brigade Headquarters was on the main street some 200m north of the canal bridge, the 16/Middlesex, commanded by **Lieutenant Colonel James Forbes Robertson**, who was to win the Victoria Cross in April 1918, was on the brigades' right flank at Mont Plaisir Farm and the canal lock bridge, the 1/Lancashire Fusiliers were on the left flank with the 2/Royal Fusiliers in support on the eastern edge of the village. The 1/RGLI was in reserve in the catacombs at the church. Le Rue Vertes, on the south side of the bridge, was split between the 29th

Lieutenant Colonel James Forbes Robertson.

and 20th Divisions and was almost completely undefended. To make matters worse, Le Rue Vertes contained 86 Brigade's ammunition and bomb dump on the La Vacquerie road, the very road the Germans were advancing along!

With Mont Plaisir Farm now driven in by the attackers, albeit with heavy casualties, the enemy advance continued south of the canal and Le Rue Vertes was entered unopposed. **Brigadier General Ronald Cheape**, commanding 86 Brigade, sent 41-year-old **Captain Robert Gee**, the staff captain responsible for the ammunition dump, to establish a defensive flank in Le Rue Vertes and **Captain Charles Loseby** to warn the 16/Middlesex at the lock. He also dispatched two 1/RGLI companies to assist in the Le Rue Vertes debacle. Stanley Blicq watched them march down the main street:

> They swung out into Masnières, cobbled hill, rifles slung, and marched with all the nonchalance in the world towards the bridge, cigarettes and pipes going, laughing and joking – thus have I a hundred times watched them go on parade. That march was a classic; let it go down in history as an emblem of the old Ten Hundred. Their last march together, their last foot chorus on the long trails. Square of shoulder, upright, I see even now those figures that have long since been still.

The RGLI regimental march was based on a Norman marching song, sung at the Battle of Hastings. Men of Guernsey, Alderney and Sark were proud to serve their sovereign and, as English was seldom their first language, they spoke a version of French found only in the Channel Islands. Today St Peter Port in Guernsey is twinned with Masnières. Incidentally, Brigadier Cheape's brother, Lieutenant Colonel Hugh Cheape, led the last cavalry charge of the British Army at Huj in the Sinai desert in November 1917 when 181 horses of the Warwickshire and Worcester Yeomanry successfully charged a force of 20,000 Turks.

From the church head downhill along Ruelle de l'Église, which runs parallel to the main street, and at the end turn left into Rue de Crèvecoeur. Stop here. At the junction of Ruelle de l'Église with Rue de Crèvecoeur glance down the main street to where the former site of 86 Brigade Headquarters was situated on the left. Behind the houses was the former chateau and its grounds. Continue along Rue de Crèvecoeur, which curves gently round to the right and after approximately 450m take the road on the right. According to trench maps the former site of the **sugar factory** was at this junction on the south side of the road, presumably where the garden of the private house now stands behind the wall. This is where Brigadier Ronnie Cheape sent a company of the RGLI to cover the left flank with machine guns. The company included **Private Latimer le Poidevin**, who recalled that, 'Our officer [Captain Harry Stranger who was awarded the MC] came and moved us and took us back over this canal and placed us in front of a sugar factory, only the top of the building was blown in and the bottom was a cellar.' The *Manchester Guardian* of 10 December 1917 was a little more explicit:

Private Latimer le Poidevin RGLI.

> We had a number of machine guns in the sugar factory ... These machine gunners under a Captain were the bulwark which largely supported the village ... A German column which must have been nearly a regiment in strength was sent from Crèvecoeur to cross the canal and attack Le Rue Vertes. It was a splendid mark for the machine gunners firing from the sugar factory across the flats and I am told that at least 500

The Fort Garry Horse Monument with the bridge over the D664 visible in the distance.

of the enemy were killed by bullets or drowned after falling wounded into the canal as they tried to cross it by a narrow bridge.

In 90m turn left down **Rue du Premier Mai** which takes you down to the **Fort Garry Horse Monument** on the canal bank ❷. The monument was unveiled in June 2004 as part of a visit by the regiment. Panels on the side of the monument explain the charge and there is also a map showing the direction of the charge and the return by Strachan and his men. A glance to the east reveals the lock over which B Squadron crossed the canal and which was later occupied by the 16/Middlesex on 30 November. On 20 November two companies of the

Lieutenant Colonel Charles Linton commanded the 4/Worcesters.

The Masnières War Memorial.

4/Worcesters crossed here and seized the trenches beyond it, near the sugar factory, organizing them for defence. At 2.00pm 36-year-old **Lieutenant Colonel Charles Linton**, commanding the battalion, went forward across the canal to see the situation for himself. On his way back, whilst crossing the lock, he was shot dead by a German sniper. He is buried at Fins New British Cemetery.

Turn right and walk along the canal bank with the canal on your left, the main road bridge is visible ahead of you. Just before the bridge on the right is the **Masnières War Memorial** ❸, which was inaugurated in October 1927. Designed by Raoul Deligne and sculptured by Pierre Delannoy, the monument was built thanks to public money and the generosity of Madame Burchard-Hostetter. There is a monument dedicated to her son Theodore near the site where his plane came down, and his body is now buried in the American Cemetery at Bony. Hostetter's monument is situated south of the canal on the right of the minor road to **Les-Rues-des-Vignes** (Chemin des Rues-des-Vignes), about 500m east of the roundabout.

The towpath connects directly with the road bridge and a left turn across the bridge will take you into Le Rue Vertes. The bridge is the modern version of the bridge that collapsed under the weight of Tank F.22 *Flying Fox II*. Apparently with some men of the Rifle Brigade

The Hostetter Memorial.

clinging to the outside, the tank started to make its way across, leaving the doors open, the tank's crew were obviously somewhat doubtful of the success of the venture and when the water engulfed them, they were able to escape ❹. Last to leave was the commander of the tank, **Second Lieutenant Walter Farrar**, who was awarded the MC for attempting the crossing. The men of the Rifle Brigade were the first to get here and cross the bridge and if you look along the canal to the right for about 500m you can get some idea of where the Newfoundland Regiment crossed from the south bank over a wooden bridge.

Captain Robert Gee VC.

As you cross the bridge look to your left and between the canal and l'Escaut is a house partly hidden by trees. This is where 86 Brigade established their Rear Brigade Headquarters on 30 November. Continue along Rue Lain for 480m to the junction with a small pathway on the right (look out for a low, single-storey private house on the right, the pathway is immediately to the left).

This is the site of **Captain Robert Gee**'s first roadblock, the defensive flank running across to the lock to where the 16/Middlesex were. The ammunition dump was two houses beyond the first roadblock and it was here that Gee bashed a man over the head and then climbed a wall into the dump. Then, after disposing of two Germans, the second being shot by the British soldier he had previously mistakenly bashed over the head, he met the two companies of 1/RGLI and proceeded to clear the street and establish a line across to the lock.

Take the pathway for 170m to the junction with **Allée des Tilleuis**, bearing right to the crossroads. This is the site of Gee's second roadblock. If you look to your left you can see the position of the German machine gun which Gee rushed, the site of which is marked today by a bus shelter. At the end of this road – Rue du Calvaire – is a small roundabout with a crucifix hidden amongst the vegetation ❺. This was the site of another German machine gun which was positioned in a corner house on the left, Gee dealing with the gun with the aid of a Stokes mortar. Robert Gee's award

The crucifix at the end of Rue du Calvaire. The Germans had a machine gun to the left of the photograph.

of the Victoria Cross was a small reward for this regular officer who was commissioned from the ranks in May 1915. He was no stranger to gallantry, in July 1916 he was awarded the MC and wounded at Beaumont Hamel, but at Masnières Gee was wounded in the knee, which effectively finished his active service career. The final part of the story involved Gee swimming the canal on the way to Marcoing after being challenged by a German sentry. An altogether extraordinary man, who died in Australia in August 1960.

Now head up Rue du Calvaire towards Masnières for 95m and stop outside the gates of the former brewery.

When the 1/RGLI marched from the catacombs down the main street they were joined by 33-year-old **Captain Patrick Booth**, the Divisional Trench Mortar Officer, and **Captain William Craib**. Their contribution to the defence of Le Rue Vertes is often overlooked but they assisted in the clearing of the north end of Le Rue Vertes. At the brewery, which was also an advanced dressing station, a section of Royal Engineers from **497 (Kent) Field Company** was asleep and captured by the advancing Germans who then proceeded up

The RGLI Memorial on Le Rue Vertes.

the road towards the bridge. It seems as if it was Patrick Booth and William Craib who were responsible for driving the Germans back down the road and releasing the captives from the brewery. Sadly, Booth was mortally wounded later in the day and died of wounds on 1 December. His posthumous award of the DSO and Craib's bar to his MC were little reward for their bravery. Booth is commemorated on the Cambrai Memorial.

Continue past the brewery gates and at the junction with Le Rue Vertes turn left, and continue for another 160m to the **RGLI Memorial** which you will see in a small car park on the right. The memorial, formed from a block of Guernsey granite, was unveiled in November 2017 and marks the sacrifice made by the RGLI during their defence of Le Rue Vertes. Nearly 600 men, about 40 per cent of the regiment, were reported killed, injured or missing during the battle.

From the memorial turn left for a few metres to the junction with Ruelle Moulin and turn left up this street, after a sharp right-hand bend you will come to the junction with Rue Lain, turn left to the bridge and stop. With the situation in Le Rue Vertes restored, the attacks on the village decreased after dark but there were two more German counterattacks over the course of the next day, and on each occasion the men of the RGLI fought their way back into the village and fierce hand-to-hand fighting was the order of the day. Blicq again:

> Savident [Private Thomas Savident] ran alone into the centre of a roadway with his Lewis Gun and poured every solitary shot in one long sweep up and down the wavering lines. Rifles cracked with the rapid reloading action of marksmen until the barrels burned hot in the hand. The Germans fell back. The Normans went forward in that reckless rush. Rues Vertes was retaken! In the outskirts of the village a number of the draft were isolated, became tangled in one bloody Mêlée with the angry retreating enemy. There was nothing for it but a fight to the death. Through the glasses they could be seen to hold off the Hun for a few brief minutes and met him in a ghastly lunging of bayonets.

About 100m beyond the bridge is **Rue des Dimeurs**, on the right of the main street. Turn right here and in 80m you will see a pathway on the left, continue along here, bearing left along the path which continues for another 200m until it reaches a junction with Rue de

The Newfoundland Caribou on the D644.

Crèvecoeur. Turn left and then right to access Ruelle de l'Église and your vehicle.

All that remains is to visit the **Newfoundland Caribou** ❻ which is reached at top of the main street. The Caribou is one of five which you can visit along the Western Front, three of which are covered in previous guidebooks in this series, and all face in the direction of the enemy. The sixth Caribou has recently been erected in Gallipoli. It is probably best to use your vehicle for this section but the hardy will, I am sure, wish to walk or ride. There is plenty of parking and if you stand with the memorial in front of you, **Masnières British Military Cemetery** ❼ is some 800m along the rough track of Chemin de Rumilly and is sited on the German defence line. The men buried here, including the fifty-nine German graves, are all from 1918 but there is one recipient of the Victoria Cross, 21-year-old **Lance Sergeant Thomas Neely** (II.B.21), who was killed on 1 October 1918 serving with the 8/King's Own (Royal Lancaster) Regiment. His award of the Victoria Cross was made four days earlier on 27 September.

Masnières was evacuated under orders on the night of 1–2 December 1917 with the 1/RGLI acting as rearguard. The last word is fittingly from Blicq, who describes the withdrawal of the RGLI: 'Then they stumbled to their feet, weak from exhaustion, exposure and hunger. The wind moaned in the trees in company with their uncertain footsteps, the still forms of brother Normans smiled up at the stars and bade them mute farewell as they came away from that sacred ground, sodden with their blood.'

Route 8
Villers-Plouich and La Vacquerie

A circular tour beginning at: the Mairie in Villers-Plouich

Distance: 3.8km/2.3 miles
Grade: Easy with some uphill sections
Suitable for: 🚶 🚲
Map: Cambrai-Bertincourt 2507 SB

General description and context: The route begins in Villers-Plouich with a short excursion to the communal cemetery and the Monument before it heads towards La Vacquerie on the former **Welsh Road**, passing and crossing the former **Surrey Road**, **Newport Trenches** and the **Corner Work**. Once in La Vacquerie the route returns to Villers-Plouich along the former **Village Road** where it meets **Fifteen Ravine British Cemetery** and concludes at the Mairie.

In spring 1917 the German Army was pursued across a devastated landscape as they withdrew towards the shelter of the Hindenburg Line. As the withdrawal closed on the previously prepared trenches German resistance stiffened, particularly in the villages where final German rearguard actions were designed to slow down the pursuing forces. Amongst these villages was La Vacquerie and Villers-Plouich, which sat on the ridges in the undulating landscape around them. These ridges were soon named by the troops who eventually captured them before the Cambrai offensive. Fusilier, Border, Welsh and Highland Ridges each bore the names of the 40th Division battalions that took them, often at considerable cost.

Villers-Plouich was captured by the 'Wandsworth' Battalion of the East Surreys on 24 April 1917 and was behind the British line on 20 November, and it was from here that the attack on La Vacquerie was launched on 20 November. Once the outer perimeter defences of Villers-Plouich had been taken at 5.30am on 24 April, the attacking troops divided into three, with 23-year-old **Captain Edward Crocker**, commanding B Company, taking the right party towards the ravine southeast of the village. Crocker was killed and the advance was temporarily held up but **Corporal 'Tiny' Edward Foster** and **Lance**

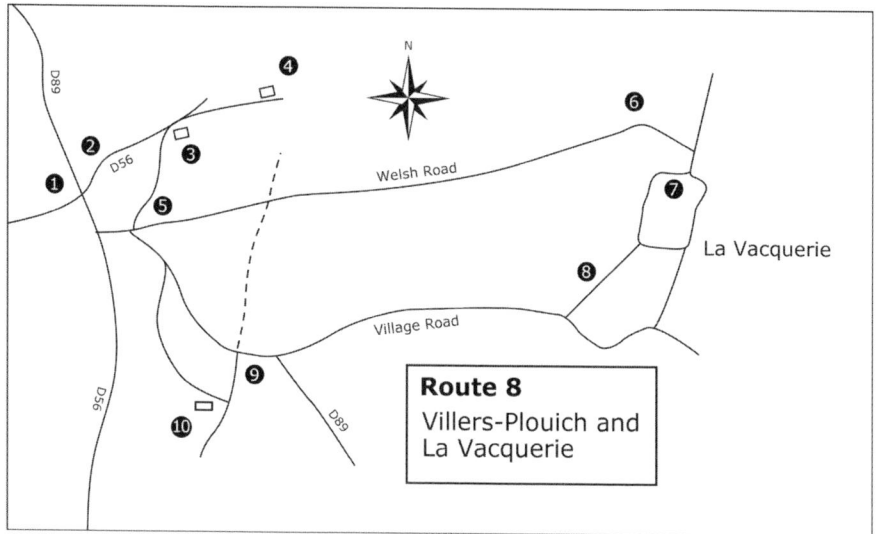

Route 8
Villers-Plouich and La Vacquerie

Corporal Reed succeeded in entering the enemy trench, knocking out the machine guns and capturing the German gun teams. Foster was awarded the Victoria Cross and Reed the DCM. The liberation of Villers-Plouich followed but at a heavy price for the 13/East Surreys, with about a third of their fighting strength lost, 39 officers and men killed and 160 wounded. Today Villers-Plouich and Wandsworth Borough Council have maintained the link established during the war and the council officially adopted the French village in 1920 when British money was used to rebuild the Mairie, this assistance recorded on the fireplace in the Mairie. Lost during the March 1918 German offensive, it is fitting that when the village was recaptured by the British in September 1918 it was liberated by the East Surreys.

Corporal 'Tiny' Foster VC.

La Vacquerie is dominated by the church and was at the front of the Hindenburg Line, jutting out rather like an arrowhead surrounded by several rows of barbed wire and deep trenches, whilst 600m away to the east were the second-line trenches which ran towards Havrincourt. Although La Vacquerie was captured early on 20 November by units of the 20th (Light) Division, it had been the subject of a large raid on 5 May 1917 involving six battalions of the 8th and 40th Divisions. The raid achieved very little and inflicted minimal damage on the German garrison and, apart from some British units gaining experience in raiding, was costly in terms of men wounded and killed. La Vacquerie was completely destroyed by this time but remained behind German lines until 20 November 1917 and was retaken again by the advancing German Army on 4 December.

Directions to start: Villers-Plouich can be approached from the south via the Bonavis crossroads on the D917 or from the north through Graincourt and Flesquières along the D89. Once in the village park near the Marie on Rue de Beauchamps.

Route description: With the Mairie ❶ on your left proceed along Rue de l'Argilliere, past the church ❷ and war memorial to reach **Villers-Plouich Communal Cemetery** ❸. There are fifty-three burials here along one wall of the cemetery and of these only eight are unidentified. The main British plot was used between November 1917 and January 1918, although it was used by the Germans in 1916. There are thirteen identified men from the Drake, Hawke and Nelson Battalions of the Royal Naval Division, all killed during the fighting on Welsh Ridge. The only officer amongst them is 29-year-old **Lieutenant Frank Purser** (B.1) of the Nelson Battalion who was

The Marie and war memorial (to the right) at Villers-Plouich.

Villers-Plouich Communal Cemetery.

killed by a sniper on 27 December 1917. The former Uppingham schoolboy went on to study at Trinity College, Cambridge, and transferred to the RND in April 1915. He is buried separately at the foot of the Cross of Sacrifice. **Captain Tom Rees** (C.2) was 21 years old when he was shot down flying as an observer in a FE.2b by Manfred von Richthofen, and was the German ace's first victory. Commissioned in January 1915, Rees was appointed Captain on 17 September 1916, the day of his death over Marcoing. Tragically, his brother David Rees was killed on the same day whilst assisting his father felling a tree. The pilot, 19-year-old **Second Lieutenant Lionel Morris**, managed to land the aircraft despite being mortally wounded and died of wounds in hospital at Cambrai. He

Captain Tom Rees.

is buried at Porte-de-Paris Cemetery, Cambrai. There is one private soldier from B Battalion Tank Corps, **S.T. Morgan** (A.7), who was killed, possibly near Marcoing, on 20 November.

From the end of the cemetery a minor road runs to the right for 450m to the **Monument** ❹, a feature that figures in the capture of the village in April 1917 and one that you may wish to drive to after the route has been completed. It can be seen on the high ground overlooking Villers-Plouich on the west and sitting on the end of the former **Surrey Road Trench**. About 700m north of the Monument was the scene of **Rifleman Albert Shepherd's**, 12/KRRC (60 Brigade), action at the junction of the Marcoing Line and the Hindenburg Line on 20 November, which gained him the award of the Victoria Cross. The ground here is featureless and there is no sign today of the mound that Shepherd attacked with B Company.

Retrace your steps from the cemetery along the pathway to the left of the road, bearing left to reach a roadway (Rue de la Garitte) after approximately 100m. The road will take you to the junction with the D89 ❺ where a right turn will take you to the start of Welsh Road. At first the road is metalled but then, after 400m, it degrades into a track.

Second Lieutenant Lionel Morris.

Rifleman Albert Shepherd VC.

The attack against La Vacquerie, which in 1917 was almost completely in ruins, went in at 6.20am between Welsh and Village roads with three waves of 61 Brigade supported by some thirty-five tanks of I Battalion. The first wave was formed by A and B Companies of the 7/DCLI on the left and the 7/Somerset Light Infantry on the right, behind them were the 12/King's Liverpools and the 7/KOYLI. Drawn up behind the tanks, the first wave of the Somersets was to capture and consolidate La Vacquerie and La Vacquerie Support, whilst the first wave of Cornwalls was tasked with capturing the

Corner Work and associated trenches. **Second Lieutenant George McMurtrie** was in the first wave with the Somersets:

> Our company was in support to B Company and when we advanced we had to follow B Company about 150 yards behind. B Company were just behind the front line. There was a large flat expanse of grass on which we assembled with a good many shell holes scattered over it. The tanks were already there and soon B Company also turned up ... No one who has ever been in an attack can forget the night before. We all looked forward to it with excitement, we were all highly strung and all of us thought – what will become of me? – I hope I do my job well – Have the enemy any knowledge of our attack?

In fact McMurtrie's fears about the enemy having knowledge of the attack were not unfounded. On the night of 18–19 November a man of 60 Brigade had fallen into enemy hands and may have inadvertently given away the whole plan, but as the regimental historian wrote later, even if the enemy discovered everything the attack would still have to be made. You can imagine that this added to the stress the attacking troops were already feeling.

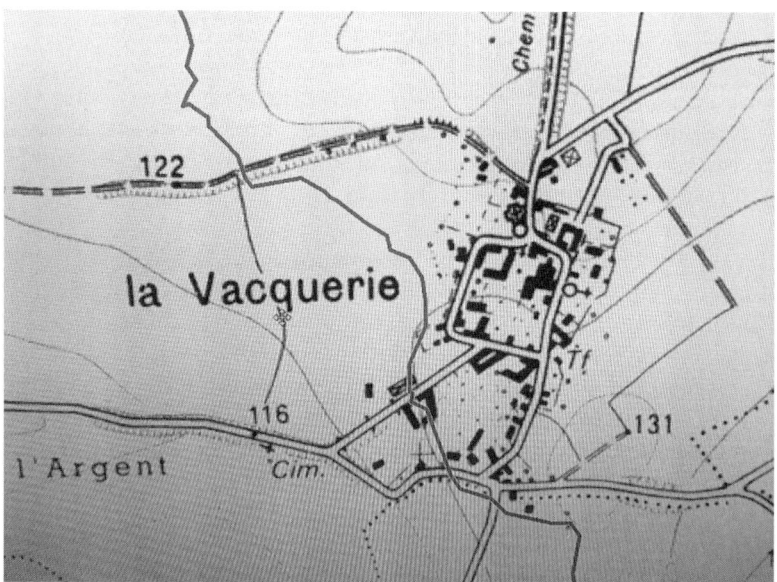

Map showing Welsh Road and Village Road and the village of La Vacquerie.

At 6.10am the first wave, led by the wire-cutting tanks, moved off and was followed by the second wave some 10 minutes later, a movement that coincided with the opening barrage. The whole of the sky seemingly turned red as the noise of shells passed over the heads of the troops to fall on the unsuspecting enemy ensuring a chaos of exploding ordnance paved the way for the advancing British. Near to **Welsh Road** George McMurtrie could see the village ahead of him:

> There was a sunken road in the side of the hill leading to La Vacquerie. So far we had been very lucky and had few casualties. By now the enemy had more or less got over the surprise and their machine gunners were beginning to be effective; bullets were whistling just over our heads. We had to keep pretty low to avoid being hit.

In the front of the advance were the tanks of I Battalion. **Captain 'Jake' Wilson**, commanding 7 Section of 25 Company which was advancing with B Company of the Cornwalls, was faced with a dilemma when the tank he was travelling in broke down:

> Having got to the enemy front line the engine conked out with water in the jets. This was the pivot tank in which I was travelling. I had to make a quick decision and ran the gauntlet to the left tank commanded by Second Lieutenant Parsons which became the pivot ... We successfully silenced any enemy machine guns that were plastering our look-out slits, paving the way for the infantry following in our wake to mop up and take La Vacquerie on our right flank almost without cost.

On Welsh Road continue past the junction with **Les Muids** (Welsh Road becomes a track after this junction) to find the former **Surrey Road**, a communication trench 160m further on, the site of the trench is marked by the track on the left which in 1917 went northeast to the Monument. Further along **Newport Trench** crosses the track and in approximately 600m you will be standing on the British front line. There is nothing to mark its position today, but it was a little over 170m from there to the first of several belts of barbed wire and the German front line, marked by Welsh Road bearing a little to the left. The defending German garrison was RIR90 and RIR19 and from all accounts it was overwhelmed quickly. Continue to the northern edge of the La Vacquerie defences where you will find the Corner Work ❻, but all that remains today is a slab of concrete with tree growing out of it.

At 7.30am the Hindenburg line was under the control of the infantry and an hour later they had taken the Hindenburg Support Line. The 7/DCLI losses on 20 November were two officers and fifty-nine other ranks wounded and nineteen other ranks killed and missing. The first prisoners coming out of La Vacquerie were, according to George McMurtrie, running as fast as they could with their heads bobbing up and down, not knowing where to go or what to do next. Although the operation went smoothly, it did leave behind the wrecks of fifteen tanks, four of them being destroyed by German artillery fire. Others had become stuck in communication trenches and I.28 *Incomparable* lost its Canadian commander, **Second Lieutenant Spencer March-Phillips**, whilst trying to cross the trenches east of the village. His name is on the Cambrai Memorial.

At the next junction turn right along **Rue Arnoult Troux de Gerville** and continue to the church ❼ which you will see on the right and stop. It was near here that George McMurtrie saw an Indian cavalryman: 'In the middle of La Vacquerie we came across an Indian cavalryman and there were already notices up about canteens and tea for the wounded. It was remarkable how soon they [presumably the support troops] had got everything in working order.' The church of Saint-Joseph de la Vacquerie replaced the ruined building that was destroyed in 1917. It was rebuilt between 1923 and 1930 and designed by Pierre Leprince-Ringuet. On the front of the building around the rose window are sculptures by Marcel Gaumont, probably completed in 1928, depicting Christ surrounded by angels. Immediately opposite the church turn left for 70m and, following the sharp bend round to the right, continue along the road for another 160m where a right turn will deliver you to the start of **Rue des Peupliers** ❽. This road is almost arrow straight and is marked by the poplar trees at the far end. At the junction turn right and stop at the village cemetery

The church at La Vacquerie.

on the left. You are now standing on **Village Road** and it is a good spot on which to consider the advance of German forces on 30 November.

During the evening of 1 December the 61st (2nd South Midland) Division relieved the 2/Grenadier Guards, 12th and 20th Divisions in the La Vacquerie sector and although Crown Prince Rupprecht had planned for another large-scale attack on the village on 3 December, the fighting did not diminish in any way. **Captain James Wyatt** of the 2/4 Gloucestershires (61st Division) was dispatched on 1 December to arrange the relief of the defending British garrison and as the 61st took over the positions in La Vacquerie all the signs pointed to an epic struggle having taken place. **Company Sergeant Major Walter Lockwood** of the 2/6 Gloucesters (183 Brigade) was amazed at the devastation that lay around him as his battalion moved up into the line:

> We moved into an area that had once been the village of La Vacquerie. The trenches were piled high with dead. It was difficult to move about in places. The whole place was a scene of complete and utter disaster. Nobody knew just what part of the trenches we were supposed to take over or exactly where the Germans were ... We did finally take over from a small party of Grenadier Guards headed by a corporal. When our commanding officer asked him where his officers were he replied very quietly, 'They are all dead, sir, we are all that is left'.

As the British were pushed back to the outskirts of the village on 3 December by GIR110 and FIR40, Lockwood and about ninety men still held on to their position but the writing was on the wall and after a heavy German attack, it was all over. La Vacquerie, what was left of it, was back under German occupation. Writing home afterwards, *Fusilier* **Karl Felber**, of FIR40, described his part in the battle:

> I leapt up with my other comrades and we raced towards the village. By the time we reached it, a few moments later, we were completely out of breath. There were bullets whistling past our ears, but nothing could stop us. In La Vacquerie itself, the British fought desperately, but a few well aimed grenades brought them to their senses or disposed of them. Moving through the village I bumped into four gunners, who simply wanted to get clear of the clouds of dust and dirt. They were not particularly courageous, because as soon as they saw me they raised their hands and started jabbering away nineteen to the dozen.

Fifteen Ravine British Cemetery.

At about 2.00pm units of the German ID185 began to arrive in the village to relieve ID28 but the battle had been something of a Valhalla for FIR40, which regarded the capture of the village as one its most outstanding achievements of the war.

Continue past the communal cemetery and along **Village Road** to pass over the British front line after approximately 500m and **Newport Trench** some 190m further on. At the junction with the D89 ❾ turn left, signposted Gonnelieu and Epehy, and turn right after 80m to find **Fifteen Ravine British Cemetery** ❿ straight ahead. The road you are walking/riding along was called **Farm Ravine** on trench maps and although the cemetery is named after Fifteen Ravine, the cemetery is in fact at the end of Farm Ravine, east of the railway line. Fifteen Ravine is a little further south of Villers-Plouich and runs at right angles to the railway line. The cemetery, sometimes referred to as Farm Ravine Cemetery, was begun by the 17/Welsh in April 1917 following the attack on Villers-Plouich and Fusilier Ridge by the 40th Division. Although the original burials lie in Plot 1, the cemetery was enlarged considerably after the Armistice when bodies were brought in from surrounding battlefields to the extent that it now contains 1,264 casualties of which over half remain unidentified, many of whom would have lain out on the battlefield for a year or more, their bodies marked only by time. There are special memorials to forty-four casualties known to be buried in the cemetery and ten Argyll and Sutherland Highlanders killed at Beauchamp on 24 April 1917 and buried in the former Argyle Road Cemetery. Eleven identified men of the 13/East Surreys involved in the attack on Villers-Plouich on 24 April 1917 can be found here, including 23-year-old **Captain Edward Crocker** (II.D.9) commanding B Company. From the 37 Brigade attack on Le Quennet Farm near Lateau Wood on 20 November are fourteen officers and men, including **Major William Alderman** (III.B.10), who was temporarily in command of the 6/Royal West Kents (RWK) in the absence of Lieutenant Colonel William Dawson, and killed along with **Lieutenant Gilbert Carré** (III.B.12) and **Lieutenant William Boucher** (III.B.13). The other ranks killed from the battalion at Lateau Wood are also buried here; amongst them is **Private Arthur Sapey** (III.B.4) from Norfolk who left his wife Ruby a widow. **Captain Alan Thomas**, the author of *A Life Apart*, wrote of the personal distress caused by Carré's death, particularly as he had warned his friend about rushing ahead of his men and not to be careless of his own safety. There are four RFC casualties, **Second Lieutenant George Young** (VII.E.14) and **Second Lieutenant Alan Wylie** (VI.E.20) were shot down by machine-gun fire flying an RE8 from 15 Squadron on 20 November 1917, whilst almost a year later **Captain Thomas Symonds** (V.C.7) and **Second Lieutenant Frank Chadwick** (V.C.8) were killed flying a 59 Squadron RE8 on 29 September 1918, being brought down near Lateau Wood.

Major William Alderman.

Lieutenant Gilbert Carré.

From the cemetery a track runs alongside the northern wall towards Villers-Plouich, bending to the right before it meets another much wider track leading to a large farm complex. Almost immediately opposite is a track which joins the D89 after 200m. Take this track and at the junction with the D89 turn left and follow the road round the bend to the left and continuing to the T-junction with **Rue Gregorie Peugniez**, where a right turn will return you to the Mairie and your vehicle.

Route 9
Gouzeaucourt and Gonnelieu

A circular tour beginning at: the Mairie at Gouzeaucourt

Distance: 7.1km/4.4 miles
Grade: Easy with some uphill sections
Suitable for: 🚶 🚵
Map: Cambrai-Bertincourt 2507 SB

General description and context: From Gouzeaucourt the route heads towards Gonnelieu on the D96, passing over the British front line and Green Switch Trench before heading north to **Gonnelieu Communal Cemetery** and the site of Captain George Paton's Victoria Cross action. Leaving the village, the route then takes the track leading southwest towards **Quentin Mill**. From the mill a short foray to **Gouzeaucourt New British Cemetery** completes the route before a return to the Mairie is made. **Gouzeaucourt** was adopted by Worcester in February 1921, who supported the town with the gift of a wind pump to supply clean drinking water to the residents, an association that was extended to the twinning of the two conurbations in 2014. Before the German counterattack of 30 November 1917 both Gouzeaucourt and Gonnelieu were behind the British front line, although both villages have had a rather chequered wartime history. Gouzeaucourt was captured by the 8th Division on the night of 12–13 April 1917 but it was lost on 30 November 1917 in the German counterattack but recaptured the same day by the 1/Irish Guards. It was lost again on 22 March 1918, attacked by the 38th (Welsh) Division on 18 September and finally retaken by the 21st Division on 8 October 1918. **Gonnelieu** was captured on 20 April 1917 by the 8th Division, lost on 30 November and only regained in 1918.

According to Jack Sheldon, the notion of a large-scale German counterattack had been proposed by German Army Group Headquarters almost as soon as the British attacks opened on 20 November and, under the direction of *General der Infantrie* **Herman von Kuhl**, his staff quickly identified the location, availability

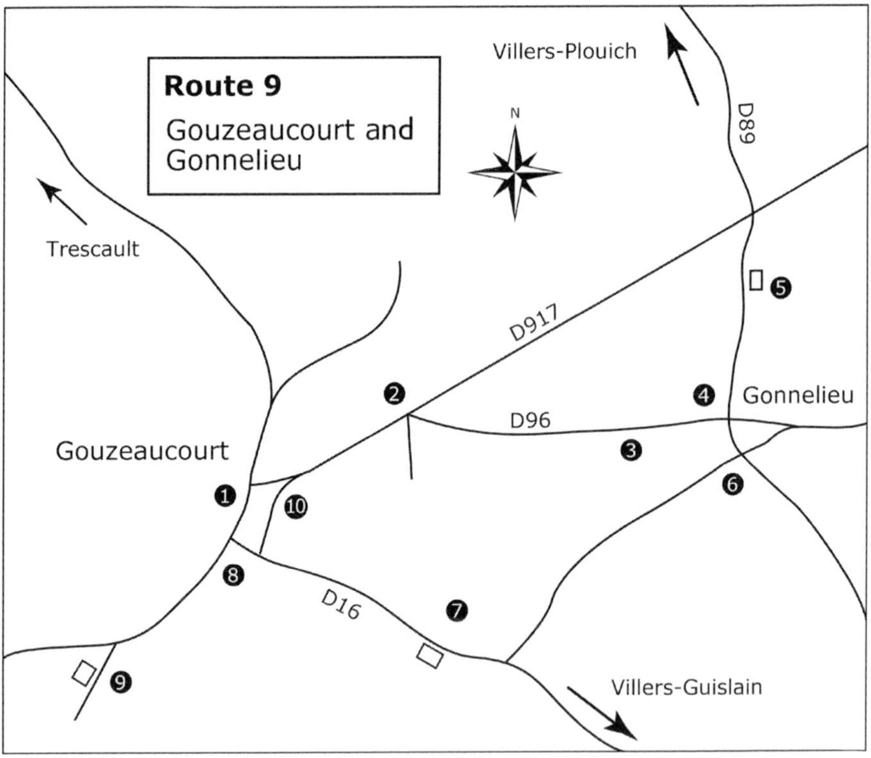
Route 9
Gouzeaucourt and Gonnelieu
Villers-Plouich
N
D89
Trescault
D917
Gonnelieu
D96
Gouzeaucourt
D16
Villers-Guislain
1
2
3
4
5
6
7
8
9
10

and transport times of reinforcements, issuing orders to ensure Second Army resources were augmented as speedily as possible. The meeting between **Crown Prince Rupprecht** and **Ludendorf** took place at the Second Army Headquarters at Le Cateau on 27 November, the Crown Prince noting in his diary on 27 November that Ludendorff and *General* von Kuhl then drove to Tournai and released orders that the counterattack would take place on 30 November.

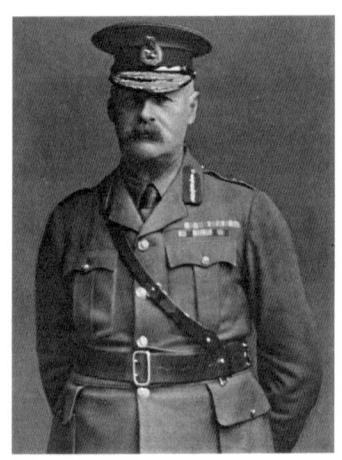

Lieutenant General Sir Thomas Snow, commander of VII Corps, 1917.

Amongst the British high command 59-year-old **Lieutenant General Sir Thomas Snow**, commanding VII Corps, was convinced that a

German counterattack would be launched opposite his corps front and even reported his concerns to Third Army, suggesting a date of 29 or 30 November for the German attack. However, British intelligence suggested the contrary and felt that German losses in Flanders and Cambrai were so severe that they precluded any counterattack. How wrong they were! VII Corps were ready for an attack from 5.30am on 30 November and, with Snow's warning ringing in Third Army ears, at 6.00am the enemy guns opened fire with high explosive and gas and an hour later German infantry began moving forward. In what appeared to be a panic stricken reply the Third Army allocated the 1st Cavalry Division to VII Corps and the 61st Division was brought forward to the sector between Metz and Heudicourt to where it could support any of the three corps. Meanwhile, on the 55th Division's left, 166 Brigade took the full force of the German attack, whilst on the right 35 Brigade (12th Division), which was southeast of Gonnelieu, came under fire at 6.45am. The 7/Suffolks, on the right of the 12th Division, were practically wiped out, only one officer and about fifty other ranks escaping with their lives. German Infantry from ID34, plus those who had been deflected from Villers-Guislain (Villers-Guislain was taken by ID34 at 8.00am), continued up the valley and advanced unopposed into Gouzeaucourt.

The fall of Gouzeaucort was a serious blow which probably woke Third Army Headquarters to the alarming weight of the German attack. No defences had been prepared outside the village and under the command of **Lieutenant Colonel Geoffrey Hayes** of the 11/DLI, contingents of the DLI, West Yorkshire and Essex Regiments withdrew toward Metz. The 1 Guards Brigade were at Metz-en-Couture under **Brigadier General Claude Champion de Crespigny** and initially assigned to support VII Corps, but as it became apparent that III Corps were also threatened, orders were received to assist III Corps. What is clear is that even with the conflicting orders that appeared to be complicating matters, the 1 Guards Brigade, with 2/Grenadier Guards (GG) in reserve, continued with their relentless advance on Gouzeaucourt. The orders detailing the Guards Brigade advance were to recapture Gouzeaucout and occupy the high ground east of the village. Reconnoitring officers had already established from the many stragglers streaming out of Gouzeaucourt that the enemy were already in possession of the village. Rudyard Kipling, in his history of the Irish Guards, writes of an 'observer of that curious day' whose comments regarding the stragglers were, at the very least, disdainful: "'Tis little ye can do with gun sights, an' them in the arums av men in a great haste. There was men with blankets round 'em, an' men with loose putties wavin' in the wind, and they told us 'twas a general retirement. We could see that.'

What appeared to have impressed the Guardsmen was the extreme openness of the ground between Gouzeaucourt Wood and the village particularly when they were machine-gunned as they topped the rise beyond the wood near Queen's Cross (see **Route 10**). What is perhaps not fully appreciated is that Champion de Crespigny deployed his men without artillery or tank support and they were machine-gunned mercilessly as they approached Gouzeaucourt along the line of the present-day D29b, with the Irish Guards to the north of the road and the 2 and 3/Coldstream Guards to the south. Overrunning a trench containing some engineers and pioneers belonging to the 20th and 29th Divisions who were still holding out (possibly Lincoln Reserve Trench), the three battalions of Guards reached the slope down into Gouzeaucourt almost at the same time as the dismounted cavalry of the 20/Hussars appeared to extend the line to the right. The Guards pushed on through the village under intense machine-gun fire and up the slope to its eastern side. **Lieutenant Frederick Salmon** of the Royal Engineers thought the Irish Guards were a stirring sight and looked as though they were in Hyde Park, marching at attention with their band playing. Whether the Germans of ID34 agreed with him is debatable. Those Germans occupying the village were expelled so rapidly that it caught many of the other British units by surprise, so much so that **Lieutenant Colonel Tom Woolocome** of the 11/Middlesex, who was ordered to counterattack Gouzeaucourt at 2.00pm that day, learnt shortly before his battalion was due to move off that the Guards had already taken the place at the point of the bayonet! In fact, by 1.30pm the Guards Brigade line ran along the western side of the former railway line and many of the British guns, captured by the Germans, were used to shell the retreating German infantry. No. 4 Company, 2/Coldstream Guards retook a supply train which was standing in the station, and this was considered most useful to the brigade as, in the urgency of going into action, there had been no proper issue of rations that day.

Working on the railway at Gouzeaucourt during the German advance were 4 officers and 280 men of the 11/American Railway Engineers together with men of the 4/Canadian Railway Troops. As soon as British troops were seen retreating over the ridge the Americans realized that this was indeed an attack in some strength. The senior officer present, Major Burbank, recognizing his men could be uselessly sacrificed, ordered a withdrawal. **Captain Raymond Hulsart** described the ensuing chaos:

Officers of the 11/American Railway Engineers at Gouzeaucourt. Left to right: Captain Raymond Hulsart, 1st Lieutenant Paul McLoud and 1st Lieutenant Holstrom. Hulsart and McLoud were decorated for their actions at Gouzeaucourt.

The men consequently became somewhat scattered, though not disorganised. Some succeeded in making their way under the command of their officers through Gouzeaucourt, some sought refuge in dug-outs from the downpour of high explosive and gas shells, whilst some rallied into an improvised unit and offered some resistance. They seized any weapons at hand, although some fought effectively with their picks and shovels until overcome.

It is not known whether any of the railway troops actually joined in with the Guards in their recapturing of Gouzeaucourt but their response, however futile, delayed the German advance along the main Cambrai–Gouzeaucourt road providing a little more time for reinforcements to be organized. According to the war diary of the 11/American Railway Engineers, several men were wounded but there were no fatalities.

At about 10.00am a call went out for all tanks in working order to be used as reinforcements. The tanks of D, E and F Battalions were dispersed through Havrincourt Wood prior to being entrained at Fins, a railhead about 3 miles south of Metz. Cobbling together ten tanks from E Battalion and seventeen from D Battalion, **Major William Watson** admitted that the tanks arrived far too late to assist the Guards: 'But the sight of the tanks on the ridge to the west of the village [Gouzeaucourt] may have assisted in the discouragement of the enemy, since he made no further effort to advance, although if he had known it, there was little enough in front of him.' Watson may have been correct about discouraging the enemy but the men of ID34 were exhausted and any further advance was perhaps out of the question. All that remained now was for the 3 Guards Brigade, under **Brigadier General Lord Henry Seymour**, to retake the village of Gonnelieu.

Major William Watson, photographed earlier in the war.

Directions to start: Gouzeaucourt is best approached via the D930 in the north. If intending to approach from the south via the Bonavis crossroads, the D917 is best. Once in the village, park near the Mairie on Avenue du Général de Gaulle.

Route description: With the Mairie on the right ❶ proceed along **Avenue du Général de Gaulle** for approximately 100m and turn right at the junction, signposted Cambrai and the A26 motorway. Continue for another 650m, passing **Place de la Gare** on the right. Along this road is the former railway station which was one of the objectives of 1 Guards Brigade and where the Welsh and Grenadier Guards of 3 Guards Brigade were dug in on the night of 30 November. In 1917 Place de la Gare was a sunken road which ran down the left of the railway tracks to the junction with the present-day D16. You can see the former railway line running across the road just before you turn right ❷ along the **Route de Gonnelieu** and if you look to your left, you will see the railway memorial. That night **Brigadier General Henry Walker**, commanding 16 Brigade (6th Division), held a conference at the 4/Grenadiers headquarters explaining that if his brigade (and 60 Brigade of the 20th Division) were unsuccessful the Grenadier and Welsh Guards would have to carry out the attack. Accordingly, the two brigades launched the

The Mairie and war memorial at Gouzeaucourt.

The former railway station on Place de la Gare.

hastily arranged operation against Gonnelieu at 1.00am and in the darkness over unfamiliar ground the 2/York and Lancs and the 1/King's Shropshire Light Infantry (KSLI) lost direction leaving a combined effort by the 6/Ox and Bucks and the 12/RB to attack the village. It failed, and when news of their abortive attack reached **Lieutenant Colonel Viscount Gort**, commanding the 4/Grenadiers, he immediately put the battalion on standby. His headquarters must have been in Gouzeaucourt as Ponsonby's history of the Grenadier Guards has the 4th Battalion crossing the Villers-Plouich road and digging in along the railway line to await zero hour.

After you have turned right, signposted Gonnelieu, on the D96, stop. Ahead of you is the ground covered by the 3 Guards Brigade in their advance on Gonnelieu. Saturday, 1 December dawned a bright day with relatively high temperatures for the time of year. The previous day the companies of the 1/GG had taken up a line along the railway between Gouzeaucourt and Villers-Plouich with No. 2 Company in touch with the 4/GG at the station. The task of the 1st Battalion was to protect the left flank as the advance continued towards Gonnelieu. The attack was to be carried out by the 4/GG on the left and the 1/Welsh Guards on the right, with the 2/Scots Guards already on the high ground on the left around Villers-Plouich. D and E Tank Battalions were supposed to support the attack but failed to arrive – the E Battalion tanks got lost and the D Battalion tanks ran out of petrol! Four tanks of H Battalion under Captain Grounds were therefore lent to the Welsh Guards. It is likely that the 4/GG used the line of the D917, which you can see to your left, but kept to the right of the road, leaving the Welsh Guards to advance to the right of the present-day D96. The tanks once more failed to turn up on time leaving the Welsh Guards, under **Lieutenant Colonel Douglas Gordon**, to move forward over Quentin Ridge on their own. **Captain Charles Dudley-Ward** watched their advance begin uphill from the railway line and doubted if they would make their objective. In this assessment he was probably correct. **Lance Corporal Charles Evans** was in the Welsh Guards advance:

> We walked up a slope at Gouzeaucourt and then we got onto a flat plateau and that's when the machine guns opened out. We had 250 casualties in the first three minutes! The three companies that suffered were Nos 2, 3 and 4; the Prince of Wales Company was in reserve down by the station.

Whilst Evans and his comrades were pinned down on Quentin Ridge, Dudley-Ward saw a lone tank, presumably of H Battalion, followed by the Prince of Wales Company, attack a trench and take some 200 prisoners. This brief respite allowed the surviving guardsman to resume their assault which ultimately failed in the face of vicious machine-gun fire. Of the remainder of the tanks two were incapacitated by mechanical difficulties and two, including the tank seen by Dudley-Ward, were destroyed by artillery fire within minutes of each other.

Continue along the D96 for a further 500m and stop. This is where **Green Switch Trench** crossed the road on its way north towards Villers-Plouich. It was somewhere around here that the Grenadiers came across the remnants of the 6/Ox and Bucks of 20th Division who had remained in situ since the abortive night attack of 30 November. The first of two Victoria Cross actions at Gonnelieu took place the previous day in the fields about 400m from the water tower, which you can see on the right of the road. There are a number of hard standings where, at the time of writing, you can pull off the road if you are driving and from where C/63 Battery, Royal Field Artillery, was positioned in the fields to the left, about 170m from the road on the morning of 30 November 1917. Firing on Honnecourt, casualties were light until at about 10.30am when enemy infantry crossed Quentin Ridge and appeared behind the battery. **Lieutenant Samuel Wallace** turned one of the guns and drove the enemy back over the ridge and continued to engage targets, notably at Gonnelieu cemetery. After

The water tower at Gonnelieu.

2 hours, with only two guns and five men remaining intact, Wallace ran the guns out of their pits and, practically surrounded by German infantry, they kept both guns in action. With almost no ammunition left, Wallace was relieved to see reinforcements from 60 Brigade arrive from the north and the guns were saved. To avoid being overrun, the headquarters of 36 Brigade (12th Division), which was to the northeast of the battery, moved back into Villers-Pouich. Wallace was awarded the Victoria Cross and survived the war, dying in 1968.

Lieutenant Samuel Wallace, commander of C/63 Battery.

Further along the road by the water tower ❸ is the approximate site of the former **Gin Trench**, stop here to admire the panoramic views to the south and west. This is also a good point at which to appreciate Gonnelieu's tactical importance and how the battle was developing. To your right, the southern sector of the village was being attacked by the Welsh Guards, who were held up by the system of trenches which followed the line of the present-day Rue du Villers-Guislain and got little further into the village. What both the 4/GG and 1/Welsh Guards did not know was that the village was filled to capacity with German troops from two divisions (probably ID34 and ID28) intent on counterattacking Gouzeaucourt. To the north of the village, your left if you are facing the village, the 4/GG attacked the village at 6.30am without tank support and little, if any, artillery support. With practically no cover they advanced across open country in the face of terrible machine-gun fire, which swept over them like a 'driving hailstorm'. No. 2 Company, under 22-year-old **Second Lieutenant Bertram Hubbard**, strayed a little too far to the right and was practically wiped out, with both Hubbard and 21-year-old **Second Lieutenant Richard Denman** being killed. No. 3 Company, under 25-year-old **Captain John Burke**, maintained its direction and sustained few casualties until it came close to the village and then had to pause to allow No. 4 Company, under 22-year-old **Captain George Paton**, to catch up. Some time after this Burke dashed into the eastern outskirts of the village followed by **Lieutenant the Hon. Alexander 'Alec' Hardinge**, who got round to the north of the village and established a Lewis gun in the communal cemetery. (Hardinge became the 2nd Baron Hardinge of Penshurst in 1944). Burke would later be killed.

Continue to the road junction and turn left along the D89 ❹, ignoring the first turning to the right, and continue along the edge of the village on **Rue de Villers-Plouich**. We will now visit the cemetery to the north of the village, 400m along this road on the right-hand side. Here you will find the single burial of **Lance Corporal Harry Abernethy** of the 4/GG, who was killed on 1 December. **Gonnelieu Communal Cemetery** ❺ is where Lieutenant Alec Hardinge set up the Lewis gun before it jammed and he and his men were overwhelmed; only he and

Lieutenant the Hon. Alexander 'Alec' Hardinge.

Gonnelieu Communal Cemetery and the single grave of Lance Corporal Harry Abernethy, 4/Grenadier Guards.

Sergeant Hull made their way back. Originally seven guardsmen were buried in the cemetery but their graves were destroyed in the 1918 fighting and are now represented by special memorials in Villers Hill British Cemetery, Villers-Guislain. Gonnelieu Communal Cemetery may be one of the least visited grave sites on the Western Front so if you are looking to place your cross of remembrance, this is the place to do it.

From the cemetery retrace your steps for 90m and stop. The second Victoria Cross, and possibly the most gallant attempt to stabilize the Grenadiers' position, involved 22-year-old **Captain George Paton** and No. 4 Company, who had reached the trench in front of the village. Paton was approximately to the right of the road almost opposite the junction on which you are now standing. With no sign of the Welsh Guards on his right it became obvious that his best plan was to hold the trench he was in so that those that had advanced into the village would have a strong supporting line to retire to. On his left there was a mixed group of engineers from 70/Field Company and 5/Northants who appeared to be wavering in the face of the German defence. Paton accordingly leapt out of his trench (possibly Gin Avenue Trench) and ran across the open ground encouraging the wavering groups to hold fast. At first, he seemed to have a charmed life as he defied the German machine-gunners but eventually he fell mortally wounded. Paton was awarded a posthumous Victoria Cross. He is also named on the family headstone in Putney Vale Cemetery and has a road named after him in Wandsworth. Soon after this Viscount Gort was severely wounded after he had come forward to Paton's trench to see for himself what was holding his battalion up, command devolving to **Major William Pilcher**. The left flank of the village was now secure thanks to Paton's efforts, but it soon became clear that the village could not be taken especially as the Germans were counterattacking and overpowering any parties who gained a foothold in the village. The 4/GG held the face of a salient with the 1/GG holding the northern flank and the 1/Welsh Guards holding the south. According to Ponsonby and others, even if the Guards had taken

Captain George Paton VC.

the village, it could not have been held due to the failure on either flank. The news of the Guards' failure filtered back to Major William Watson of D Battalion:

> The news was disquieting. The Grenadier Guards had not been able to force an entry into the village, while the Welsh Guards on their right had made little progress. Both battalions had lost almost all their officers ... tanks could be seen on the slopes of the hill. Two silhouetted against the skyline were burning fiercely. Of my own tanks nothing could be heard ... Then came a grave rumour: The Colonel [Viscount Gort] is badly wounded! But a moment later he walked into the dugout, his arm in a rough sling and his face drawn with pain.

It had been a very costly advance for the Grenadiers, who later recorded 10 officers and 195 other ranks killed or wounded. They remained and clung on to the outskirts of Gonnelieu until 2–3 December when they were relieved by the 2/Scots Guards. The village was retained by the Germans until September 1918 when it was recaptured by the Lincolnshire Regiment.

Turn left along **Rue du Calvaire** to reach the four-way intersection on the D96. Our route lies along **Rue Jules Elby** (Elby was a French industrialist and Democratic Republican Alliance politician who represented Pas-de-Calais in the Senate between 1923 and 1933), which is almost directly opposite you. After 200m cross over **Rue de Villers-Guislain** and continue along the track ❻ leading southwest towards the D16. Ahead of you is Gauche Wood and the small copse surrounding Quentin Mill.

As you walk across the open ground of Quentin Ridge, Gouzeaucourt is on your right, as is the ground the 1/Welsh Guards advanced over. Consider for a moment the lines of men walking without a shred of cover into the machine-gun fire of the Germans at Gonnelieu. Not for nothing were the members of the Guards Division considered by many to be amongst the most disciplined men of the BEF. Continue for just over a kilometer to the junction with the D16. Directly ahead of you is a continuation of the track and some 500m from where you are standing is the former site of **Quentin Redoubt**, a feature that was constructed after the Cambrai offensive and was garrisoned by the 21st Division on 21 March 1918.

Turn right along the D16. The road now goes uphill until it reaches the site of **Quentin Mill** ❼ on the left – Ferme Capelle on IGN maps.

Quentin Mill looking from the direction of Villers-Guislain.

In conjunction with the attack on Gonnelieu, the 1 Guards Brigade were ordered to advance on Quentin Mill and Gauche Wood. The junction between the 3 Guards Brigade at Gonnelieu and the 1 Guards Brigade further south on the Quentin Ridge was approximately north of the D16 Gouzeaucourt–Villers-Guislain road with zero hour being set at 6.30am. Attacking Quentin Mill, the 3/Coldstream Guards and four tanks of H Battalion, under the command of **Captain William Gerrard**, had little difficulty in gaining their objective. **Captain Daniel Hickey** wrote afterwards that Gerrard had attacked east of Gouzeaucourt at the same time as he had attacked Gauche Wood: 'All Gerrard's tanks had been disabled, three having been knocked out. The attack proved to be "Hermosa's" last fight, and she had come to a gallant end. Brown [2/Lt William Brown], her voluntary commander, and four of her crew had met their death and the other three had been severely wounded.'

Major General Beauvoir de Lisle.

Gerrard's tanks, apart from H.27 *Hermosa*, were H.28 *Hadrian*, H.29 *Havoc II* and H.23 *Hong Kong*. They were the first tanks to enter Fontaine on 21 November, *Hadrian* being Daniel Hickey's tank.

As you draw level with Quentin Mill consider for a moment the chaos brought about by the German counterattack of 30 November as **Major General Beauvoir de Lisle**, commanding the 29th Division, had to exit very quickly to avoid being captured. He later stated that he ordered his headquarters staff to run for it:

> As we got away and were running down the road to Gouzeaucourt, a machine gun opened up on us from the hill behind at a range of 500 to 600 yards. This was unpleasant and I lost my GSO3, who was killed and several were wounded; but the most unpleasant of all was the fire from two low flying aeroplanes, less than 150 feet up. It was not easy to run that mile, and my ADC, Captain Nickalls, was soon 'all in' and required all the encouragement I could render to continue the struggle.

It would appear that seven members of the 29th Divisional Signal Company were amongst the men also killed on 30 November at Quentin Mill and were buried in the quarry, begun by the 2/RB in April 1917, close to the mill. Three of those men are now buried at Gouzeaucourt New British Cemetery. As far as de Lisle is concerned, he eventually settled down in the cellars of the Villers-Plouich Mairie.

Continue past Quentin Mill and with Gouzeaucourt ahead of you stop at the raised banks on the right of the road. This appears to be the site of an extension to the original Gouzeaucourt New British Cemetery and where three men of the 29th Divisional Signal Company were buried before being re-interred in 1919. Cross over the former railway line and turn left by the church ❽ onto the D917, signposted Epehy and Fins. This road is a

The church at the corner of Rue Villers-Guislain and Avenue du Général de Gaulle.

Gouzeaucourt New British Cemetery.

continuation of Avenue du Général de Gaulle and after 550m turn left onto the Rue d'Heudicourt where a green and white sign directs you to the **Gouzeaucourt New British Cemetery**. You will find the cemetery ❾ on the left, opposite the communal cemetery. This is a large cemetery that contains men who were killed in the Cambrai offensive as well as 1918. Begun in November 1917 and used briefly by the Germans in 1918, the original burials are to the right of the entrance, the vast remainder were brought in from cemeteries in the surrounding battlefields of Cambrai. The cemetery now contains 1,295 burials of which 381 are unidentified. A number of special memorials near the Cross of Sacrifice commemorate 35 casualties known or believed to be buried in the cemetery. The cemetery contains 113 men who were killed in 1917 with 81 being killed during the German counterattacks on 30 November and 1 December. Three members of the 29th Division Signal Company, who were killed at Quentin Mill, are buried in Row VIII, **Sapper Cuthbert Nicholson** (VIII.G.11), 37-year-old **Sergeant Edward 'Ted' Smith** (VIII B.9) and **Lance Corporal Robert Annan** (VIII.B.7). Seven soldiers of the 4/GG are buried here, **Captain John Burke** (X.A.3), commanding No. 3 Company, who was mortally wounded at Gonnelieu on 1 December, and 22-year-old **Second Lieutenant Bertram Hubbard** (Sp. Mem. A2), commanding No. 2 Company, who was killed on the same day at Gonnelieu. Attacking the same village further to the south was the 1/Welsh Guards and eight identified men of that

The British Bunker on Rue de l'Est.

battalion are buried here, including 30-year-old **Captain Hume Roderick** (X.A.1), commanding No. 3 Company. Two members of the Tank Corps rest here, 23-year-old **Private Joseph Tattershall** (II.E.10) of B Battalion, who was killed on 1 December, and **Second Lieutenant Gilbert Phillips** (III.A.3) of F Battalion, who died of wounds at Gouzeaucourt after F.49 *Fairy II* was hit on 20 November.

From the cemetery turn right and retrace your steps along the D29 to the junction with the D917. Cross straight over and continue along **Rue d'Enfer** for 450m and turn right into **Rue Solave** which will bring you back to the church after 150m. A left turn will take you back to your vehicle at the Mairie. After you have been reunited with your vehicle you may wish to visit the British Bunker on **Rue de l'Est** ❿ which is immediately behind the Mairie. If you go back to the church and turn left, Rue de l'Est is first on the right.

Route 10
Car Tour

A circular tour beginning at: the Cambrai Memorial at Louveral and concluding at Ribécourt

Distance: 56km/35 miles, depending on how much of the route you take advantage of
Suitable for: 🚲 🚗
Map: Cambrai-Bertincourt 2507 SB

Directions to start: Bearing in mind most battlefield tourists will either stay in Cambrai or travel from as far afield as Arras, the best starting point would be the **Cambrai Memorial at Louveral** on the D930 where there is ample parking.

The Cambrai Memorial at Louveral.

Route Description: The car tour is designed so that the tourist can join at any point along the way and has been designed purely as a basis for further exploration. Where the route invades the walking and cycling routes, which it does on several occasions, be aware that I have not included cemetery information where it had already been featured in a specific route and references to specific routes are included throughout the tour. Start at the Cambrai Memorial, Louveral on the D930 and go through Boursies and continue to **Demicourt Communal Cemetery** after which a left-hand turning will take you onto the D34b. Cross the D930 with care and continue to Mœuvres and **Mœuvres Communal Cemetery Extension** (see **Route 3**). Return to the staggered crossroads and continue straight ahead along Rue du Cuquiche towards the Canal du Nord. At Lock 5 on the D34a where McReady-Diarmid won his Victoria Cross on 30 November by counterattacking on the Mœuvres side of the canal some 450m south of the bridge.

Mœuvres British Cemetery on the D34a contains men who were all killed in 1918.

Continue across the canal to the junction with the D15 where a right turn will take you back across the D930. Drive parallel to the Canal du Nord on the D15 for approximately 1km and turn left

Anneux British Cemetery.

along Rue d'Hermies to **Graincourt**. Before you do, spare a moment to remember the death by shellfire of **Brigadier General Roland Bradford** at Lock 7 whilst resting with 186 Brigade in the dry canal on 30 November. Drive through Graincourt (see **Route 4**), visiting the church and the communal cemetery where Roland Bradford established his initial headquarters. Continue over the motorway to Anneux and at the crossroads at the end of the village turn left along Rue de la Chapelle, heading back towards the D630 (essentially the same road as the D930 but is now the called the D630). At the junction Anneux Chapel is straight across and **Anneux British Cemetery** is to the right (see **Route 6**).

Bourlon is along the D16 which skirts the western edge of the wood and is almost directly across from the junction of Rue de la Chapelle with the D630. It is strongly recommended that you plan your route in Bourlon on **Google Earth** before embarking on the sights of the village. Follow the D16 into the village, noting the Avenue du Bois on your right, and visit the church on Rue de l'Église with its memorial to **Lieutenant Graham Lyall**, who was awarded the Victoria Cross in September 1918. Continue to the former railway station building almost opposite the communal cemetery in the north of the village. Although the building has long been demolished, the site remains as an open area on the right-hand side of the road, as does the former trackbed which you can still see heading towards Fontaine and Cambrai. This was the scene of the final stand of the three companies of the 14/HLI (see **Route 6**).

Leave the site of the former railway station buildings and retrace your steps past the communal cemetery to the fork in the road. Turn right here and then, after 70m, turn left. If you carry straight ahead along **Rue de l'Abbaye** you will see a green and white signpost, pointing the way along a pathway to **Bourlon Wood Cemetery** which is composed entirely of 1918 burials. If you wish you can leave your vehicle and walk along the pathway to the cemetery. The track running behind the cemetery – **Chemin de Cambrai** – leads back towards the village and the **Canadian Memorial**, but the Canadian Memorial is also signposted from the top of **Avenue**

Lieutenant Graham Lyall VC.

Bourlon Wood Cemetery.

du Bois which you pass on the D16 on your way into the village, and although the memorial is dedicated to the Canadian troops who took Bourlon in September 1918, it is still worthy of a visit. There is also a memorial here to the French resistance members who were murdered in 1940. The monument is erected on ground donated by

Bourlon Wood Canadian Memorial.

the Compte de Franqueville, who was Mayor of Bourlon in 1918, and is similar in type to that at Courcelette on the Somme and Crest Farm at Passchendaele, being composed of the standard block of white Quebec granite.

Leave the memorial via **Rue du Marais** and return to the D16, pausing at the water tower and television mast where the Canadian Memorial was once intended to be erected. Continue down the D16 to the junction with the D630, turning left to **Anneux British Cemetery** on the right. From the cemetery the dark mass of Bourlon Wood is seen on the left and where several British battalions first entered the wood. The track running into the wood towards the abandoned quarry, 700m from Anneux Cemetery, is where **Lieutenant Colonel James Plunkett's** 19/Royal Welch Fusiliers entered the wood accompanied by the tanks of G Battalion on 23 November.

Continue along the D630 into **Fontaine**, turning left into Rue Roger Salengro (2.4km from Anneux Cemetery) at the crossroads on which the Mairie stands. Bear right into **Rue de la République** to reach a five-way intersection after 200m and continue along **Avenue de la Gare** to find the former station building on the right (see **Route 5**). This is the building that **Lieutenant Colonel John Unthank** of the 4/Seaforth Highlanders occupied for a short time having arrived with his battalion after Captain Daniel Hickey's four tanks had captured the village.

The former railway station at Fontaine.

Retrace your steps to the Mairie and cross straight over the crossroads along **Rue de la Liberté** to the church. On 23 November, during the second assault on Fontaine, Rue de la Liberté became the scene of a dramatic rescue between the disabled tank C.47 *Conqueror II* and C.48 *Caesar*. Hit by a unit of RIR52 using armour-piercing ammunition, C.47 was brought to a halt near the church with its commander, **Second Lieutenant Willie Moore**, seriously wounded. C.48 stopped near the wreck and, despite being under enemy fire, **Private Green** got out and helped evacuate *Conqueror's* crew and **Private Raffel** assisted the wounded Moore. Only when all eight crew members were safely on board did C.48's commander, **Second Lieutenant Archibald**, give the order to leave. For this action Archibald and Moore received the Military Cross, Green the DCM and Raffel the MM. Behind the church is a small road leading directly to the communal cemetery – please make an effort to visit the three headstones just inside the gate, against the wall, two are unidentified Seaforth Highlanders and the third is completely unknown.

From the path leading to the cemetery turn right to the junction with Rue Paul Bert where another right turn will take you to a junction with the D142. Turn left here towards Cantaing. The D142 is the sunken road along which **Lieutenant Hon. Arthur Kinnard** took D Company of the 1/Scots Guards towards Fontaine on 27 November and where he was mortally wounded on the Fontaine side of the motorway bridge, about 400m short of the modern pumping station. **Sergeant John McAuley** then took his company commander back to the safety of a dugout and took charge of the company, beating off several German attacks and leaving some fifty Germans dead. For this feat he was awarded the Victoria Cross. Kinnard is buried at **Ruyaulcourt Military Cemetery**. Just left of the road, on the Cantaing side of the motorway bridge and to the north of the junction of **Le Haut de l'Escafotte** with the D149, was the scene of another Victoria Cross action on 30 November involving **Lance Corporal John Thomas** of the 2/5 North Staffordshires. Battalion Headquarters was at Cantaing Mill and, observing the enemy preparing for another assault from the direction of Folie Wood, Thomas ran forward across the road to a dugout which was used by the Germans to concentrate their troops. Shooting three snipers and dealing with the Germans in the dugout, he returned, bringing back valuable information on enemy dispositions enabling the artillery to break up the attack.

Continue along the D142 until you reach the crossroads with the D92. To the left is **Cantaing Military Cemetery**, all 1918 casualties, and **Folie Wood**, which was never captured by the British and remained a thorn in the side of the British during the campaign. A short drive along the D92 will take you to Folie Wood with its empty and elaborate gatehouse.

At the crossroads with the D92 turn right along the main street of Cantaing, passing the church on the left, until you arrive at the crossroads with a small green on the left. The road opposite leads to a memorial dedicated to Ewart Mackintosh and is in the direction of the motorway along **Rue d'Anneux**. After 600m you will come to a junction of tracks, the site of the German strongpoint of **Cantaing Mill**.

Retrace your steps along Rue d'Anneux and turn right, bearing right again at the fork towards the water tower. At the junction with the D15 turn left to reach **La Justice** after 200m. In 1917 there was a crossroads at La Justice which the building of the motorway reduced to a T-junction. **Captain Daniel Hickey** remembered the crossroads well as, apart from the collection of farm buildings and a knocked out German battery, there was a well-constructed dugout:

> An excellent staircase some twenty steps or more led down into it ... One side of the dugout was fitted with tiers of bunks made of rabbit wire; while at the far end was a wooded partition, separating it from the farm cellars ... The left gun of the battery had been knocked out by a direct hit, a proof of the amazing accuracy of our artillery.

The entrance to Orival Wood Cemetery.

At La Justice go straight on under the A26 autoroute on the D89 to **Orival Wood**, which you will see on the right just before **Orival Wood Cemetery**. Bordered by the road, the cemetery was begun in November 1917 and used again in September and October 1918. Enlarged in 1930 by the transfer of graves from the surrounding battlefields there are now nearly 300 casualties commemorated at this site including a number of German casualties. Of these, ten are unidentified and others, identified collectively but not individually, are marked by headstones bearing the superscription 'buried near this spot'. This is very much a 1917 cemetery with over 200 men killed or died of wounds between 20 November and 6 December 1917. Four members of the Tank Corps are buried here, all killed on 20 November. The three men from D Battalion, 24-year-old **Private John Walker** (I.B.15), 23-year-old **Lance Corporal Frederick Knight** (I.D.4) and 19-year-old **Private James Murphy** (I.A.1) are buried close to 27-year-old **Private David Chidgley** (I.C.16) of E Battalion, who hailed from Bristol. These men may have been originally buried at **Flesquières Chateau Cemetery** – now defunct – and probably took part in the tank battle at Flesquières. There are thirty-five men of the Seaforths killed in the attacks on Fontaine, amongst them 24-year-old **Captain 'Ray' MacDonald** (I.A.7), 1/4 Seaforth Highlanders, who was brought back to Cantaing from the outskirts of Fontaine after leading the assault on Cantaing Mill. Nearby is 21-year-old **Second Lieutenant Harold Wilks** (II.C.14), who was killed on 30 November 1917 serving with the North Staffordshire Regiment. Plot 1 contains thirty-seven Gordon Highlanders, probably killed alongside their fellow Seaforths. Amongst them is 37-year-old **Captain George Minty** (I.A.4), 1/6 Gordon Highlanders, the former headmaster of Inverkeithny Public School. Originally from Aberdeen, he was commissioned as a second lieutenant in 1914 and killed on 23 November. Another aging soldier was 52-year-old **Brevet Major Greville Bagot-Chester** (II.A.13), 2/Scots Guards. Known as 'Bubbles' to his friends, he was killed on 28 November. He is flanked on one side by **Private John Dawson** (II.A.12), 153/

Second Lieutenant Harold Wilks, who served with the North Staffordshire Regiment.

Machine Gun Corps, who was killed on 20 November. Last, but by no means least, is **Lieutenant Ewart Mackintosh** (I.I.26), 1/4 Seaforth Highlanders, the poet whose work appears at the front of this volume. He was killed on 21 November attacking **Cantaing Mill** along with **Sergeant John Ross** and his platoon of 1/4 Seaforths. Ross later died of wounds and is thought to be buried at **Wancourt British Cemetery**.

From the cemetery retrace your steps to La Justice and turn right to a crossroads where another left turn will take you back to **Cantaing**. Drive through the main street and turn right along the D142 to Noyelles.

Four tanks from A Battalion, A.41 *Autogophasta*, A.42 *Atlantic*, A.44 *Ahmed II* and A.45 *Astica*, having first attacked Nine Wood, advanced into the west

Lieutenant Ewart Mackintosh.

One of the bunkers at Noyelles-sur-Escaut.

of Noyelles where several machine guns were eliminated. Soon afterwards a patrol from 16/Middlesex (29th Division) entered the village and consolidated their position. A German counterattack followed on 21 November from the east. German infantry got as far as the church on Rue Pasteur and into the chateau grounds, but with the help of a squadron of dismounted 9/Lancers and the 2/Fusiliers, the village was once again in British hands by nightfall.

Continue into Noyelles and stop on the village outskirts. On the right you will see a number of gated **German bunkers** together with an information board. The bunkers were used as a barracks and ammunition store. Continue for approximately 150m to **Noyelles-sur-Escaut Communal Cemetery**, which you will see on your right, and stop. There is plenty of parking. There is only one man buried here in the bottom left-hand corner of the cemetery, 26-year-old **Lieutenant Wilfrid Cramb**, a third-year medical student from Glasgow University who was shot down flying a 9 Squadron BE2f on 14 April 1917. Cramb had been flying for just six weeks when he was killed, while his observer, **Second Lieutenant Harle**, was taken prisoner. The **Communal Cemetery Extension**, which you can see on the far side of the hedge, is made up of burials from September and October 1918 when once again Noyelles became a battleground.

The entrance to Noyelles-sur-l'Escaut Communal Cemetery.

Continue through the village on the D29 **Rue de Marcoing**, passing **Nine Wood** on the right, until the outskirts of Marcoing are reached. **Marcoing Communal Cemetery** is best approached by remaining on the D29 and turning right by the church into Rue de l'Égalité. The war graves are located within two plots in the centre of this relatively small cemetery (see **Route 7**).

Retrace your route to the junction with the D29, turn left and then immediately right along the D15 – signposted Masnières and Cambrai – bearing left at the roundabout along **Rue Roger Salengro**. This road will take you to **Rue de la Gare** on the right from where it is a simple matter to cross the canal and park in the disused railway station, the scene of **Sergeant Charles Spackman's** Victoria Cross action. If you wish to see the disused railway bridge, it will be necessary to leave your vehicle and walk across the canal bridge and turn left along the towpath in the direction of Masnières for approximately 400m.

Retracing your steps to your vehicle, leave the station and turn sharp left along the D15. From here the road sweeps round to the left to arrive at **Marcoing British Cemetery** (see **Route 7**). From here you may wish to walk along to where **Captain Arthur Lascelles** won his Victoria Cross. Leave the cemetery and continue into Masnières,

Newfoundland Caribou at Masnières.

passing straight across the roundabout to the junction with the D644 where a left turn will take you to the Newfoundland Caribou. Retrace your steps down the main street, pausing at the rather grand French Memorial and over the bridge where F.22 *Flying Fox II* crashed through the bridge into the canal. Cross the canal into Le Rue Vertes. Of course, you may wish to spend more time in Masnières exploring the various memorials such as those of the RGLI and the Fort Garry Horse as well as the rearguard action by **Captain Robert Gee** and the 1/RGLI in Le Rue Vertes, in which case **Route 7** should be further consulted. Leave Masnières and Le Rue Vertes on the D644 to the roundabout and continue straight ahead towards Bonavis. The first stop is at **Le Quennet Farm**, where it is possible to park off the main road.

In 1917 the farm was fortified by the Germans and it was left to the 6/Royal West Kents (RWK) of the 12th Division to clear Lateau Wood and 'mop up' Le Quennet and Pan Pan farms. The attack began at 6.20am on 20 November with twenty tanks of F Battalion, although there was little fighting until Pan Pan Farm was reached. Here the Germans put up a fight and it was only after the tanks had overcome them that the 6/RWK reached Lateau Wood and Le Quennet Farm at about 10.00am. The farm was lost on 30 November when 59 Brigade (20th Division) was overwhelmed in the German counterattack and was the scene of **Lieutenant Colonel Lionel Troughton's** capture. Troughton was an English amateur cricketer who played first-class cricket for Kent County Cricket Club and who was awarded the MC in September 1916.

Continue to the three-way intersection, passing **Lateau Wood** on the left, and park by Bonavis Farm on the left, taking care to follow the lane directions.

Pan Pan Farm is almost opposite the Bonavis Farm buildings on the D917 which were largely burned down in 1914 by the Germans in reprisal for a French ambush. The farm was cleared on 20 November by the 6/East Kents (Buffs) with the assistance of ten tanks, the defenders only surrendering when the farm buildings caught fire, but on 30 November the German counterattack by RIR190 recaptured it, despite 37 Brigade's resolute defence. The Buffs also encountered stiff fighting at Bonavis Farm on 20 November but were assisted by the 6/Queens who came up on the left and joined in the fight. Lateau Wood was cleared by Major Alderman and the 6/RWK but the casualties were heavy, **Major William Alderman**, **Lieutenant Gilbert Carré**, **Second Lieutenant Charles Clark** and **Lieutenant William Boucher** were all killed and **Lieutenant Siebel** badly wounded along with over eleven other ranks killed or wounded. (Alderman, Clark, Carré and Boucher are buried at **Fifteen Ravine British Cemetery** at Villers-Plouich.) On 30 November the 6/RWK Battalion Headquarters was on the reverse slope of a hill behind Lateau Wood and was eventually overwhelmed by the sheer numbers of German infantry:

> The Germans came pouring on in masses like a Bank Holiday crowd. Those in front the Headquarters party had promptly shot down, but almost immediately grey figures began emerging from Lateau Wood more to the right, and the post was before long practically surrounded and its garrison overpowered. Captain Hodgeson-Smith was twice wounded, the second time very badly, and taken, and only a few got away.

Stay on the D917, passing on the left the site of another Victoria Cross rearguard action on 30 November, that of **Lieutenant Colonel Neville Elliott-Cooper.** His action took place on the featureless terrain between Bleak House and Bonavis Farm. Just before the

The memorial to Lieutenant Colonel Neville Elliott-Cooper at Sandhurst.

Bleak House seen from the road.

motorway bridge on the right is **Bleak House**, which was captured by the 8/Royal Fusiliers on 20 November. **Second Lieutenant Jim Davies** remembers taking the farm which, for some reason, had not been shelled by the heavy artillery but eventually fell to the tanks of C and F Battalions and infantry working together.

Go over the A26 autoroute passing another former fortified building – **Les Baraques** – on left before the turning to **La Vacquerie** on the right. La Vacquerie is a small, hilltop village and was connected to the main Hindenburg Line by deep trenches and redoubts which crossed the southern end of Welsh Ridge. The task of the 7/DCLI was to capture the **Corner Work** whilst the 7/Shropshire Light Infantry (SLI) were tasked with taking the church in the centre of the village (see **Route 8**). By 10.00am the first objectives had been taken.

Drive through La Vacquerie to visit the **Corner Work**, a left turn after the church will see you and your vehicle near to the redoubt, a short walk may be necessary to reach it. Retrace your steps to the church where a right turn along Le Rue Vertes will take you to **Rue des Peupliers**. Pass the communal cemetery on the left and continue along the minor road, turning left at the junction with the D89 and then almost immediately right to **Fifteen Ravine British Cemetery** at Villers-Plouich. Should you wish to visit the communal cemetery at Villers-Plouich you will find it on the D56 on the northern outskirts of the village.

The CWG signpost for Fifteen Ravine British Cemetery.

From Fifteen Ravine British Cemetery retrace your steps to the D89 and turn right to the junction with the D917, cross straight over and stop on the left at **Gonnelieu Communal Cemetery**. This is where you will find the single burial of **Lance Corporal Harry Abernethy** of the 4/GG, who was killed on 1 December and where **Lieutenant Alec Hardinge** set up the Lewis gun before it jammed and he and his men were overwhelmed.

Continue along the outskirts of the village on the D89, past the position of **Captain George Paton's** Victoria Cross action. Paton, a 4/Grenadier Company Commander, was approximately to the right of the road almost opposite the junction of the D89 with Rue du Calvaire and Rue de la Vacquerie. The junction with the D96 – signposted Gouzeaucourt – is some 220m further on where a right turn will take you to the water tower where **Gin Trench** crossed the road. Stop here to admire the panoramic views over the battlefield to the south and west. Continue to where **Lieutenant Samuel Wallace** and the guns of C/63 Battery were positioned in the fields to the right of the road almost directly opposite some hard standings on either side of the road. Wallace was awarded the Victoria Cross on 30 November for maintaining fire with the remaining guns of C/63 Battery on the advancing Germans (see **Route 8**).

Queen's Cross with Gouzeaucourt Wood in the background.

Continue along the D96 to the junction with the D917 where there is a monument to the former railway. Turn left, crossing the former railway line, and drive along **Avenue du Général de Gaulle** for 660m and take a left turn – signposted Ephey, Villers–Guislain and Péronne. Pass the Mairie on the left and from here it is approximately 1km to **Gouzeaucourt New British Cemetery** (see **Route 9**).

From the cemetery retrace your steps to the junction, crossing straight across to Rue d'Enfer to take the minor road – Rue de Poitieres – on the left after 300m. You will quickly come to a road junction on the right, carry on straight ahead along the D29b to reach the crossroads of **Queen's Cross**. The road you have travelled along is the route taken by the 1 Guards Brigade under **Brigadier General Claude Champion de Crespigny** on their way to recapture Gouzeaucourt. The orders detailing the Guards Brigade advance were to recapture Gouzeaucout and occupy the high ground east of the village. Reconnoitering officers had established from the many stragglers streaming out of Gouzeaucourt that the enemy was already in possession of the village. Note the extreme openness of the ground between **Gouzeaucout Wood** and the village, particularly when they were machine-gunned as they topped the rise beyond the wood near Queen's Cross. What is perhaps not fully appreciated is that Champion de Crespigny deployed his men without artillery or tank support and they were machine-gunned mercilessly as

Metz-en-Couture Communal Cemetery British Extension.

they approached Gouzeaucourt along the line of the present-day D29b, with the Irish Guards to the north of the road and the 2 and 3/Coldstream Guards to the south (see **Route 9**).

Drive straight across **Queen's Cross** and through Gouzeaucourt Wood, where I and F Battalions of the Tank Corps waited prior to the offensive beginning on 19–20 November, to **Metz-en-Couture Communal Cemetery British Extension**, which you will see on the left. Park in the Communal Cemetery and walk the last few metres to the British Extension. The Communal Cemetery was used by the Germans and also for three RFC Officers, whose graves have now been removed to the British Extension. On the east side of it a German Extension was made containing the graves of 252 German soldiers and one man of the Chinese Labour Corps; the German graves have now been removed to other cemeteries and the Chinese grave to the British Extension. The British Extension was begun in April 1917 and used until March 1918. These original burials, made by field ambulances and fighting units, are in Plots I and II; Plots III and IV were added after the Armistice by the concentration of graves from local battlefields. The cemetery contains 72 men who were killed during the Cambrai offensive between 20 November and 7 December 1917 and a number of men who died of wounds afterwards, making a total of nearly 500 casualties commemorated in the cemetery and of these, almost 50 are unidentified. Special memorials record the names of four soldiers buried in the former **Metz-en-Couture British Cemetery No. 2** whose graves could not be found after the Armistice. Thirteen men of the 24/London Regiment (47th Division), who were killed on the first day of the German Spring Offensive of 21 March 1918, were obviously brought in from the Ephey area after the Armistice. Of these, **Private George Baldwin** (III.F.17), 31-year-old **Private John Beall** (IV.D.15) and 35-year-old **CQMS Alexander Horne** (III.A.17) were all probably from B Company. There are also two soldiers of the 4/GG killed during the advance on Gonnelieu, 22-year-old **Captain George Paton VC** (II.E.24) was killed on 1 December and is buried next to 21-year-old **Lieutenant Richard Denman** (II.E.23), who died of wounds on 2 December. The commander of 12/Company, D Battalion, 36-year-old **Major Robert Ward** (III.C.3), lies near to 29-year-old **Private Leonard Simmins** of D Battalion in Plot 2 D.12, both men were killed on 20 November. Two members of G Battalion lie nearby, 26-year-old **Private Henry Prescott** (II.D.17) was killed or died of wounds on 21 November and **Private Francis Redfern** (II.D.19) was killed on 20 November. This is also the resting place of 29-year-old **Lieutenant Commander Patrick Shaw-Stewart VC** (II.E.1), the temporary commander of the Hood Battalion who was killed on Welsh Ridge on 30 December along with 31-year-old **Commander Charles Skeffington** (II.F.6), commanding the Howe Battalion, who lies next to his second in command, 32-year-old **Lieutenant Commander Alan Campell** (II.F.5). **Corporal Harry Nutter**, aged 32 (II.D.2), 190 Brigade Machine Gun Company RND, also killed on Welsh Ridge on 30 December, lies nearby.

Leave the cemetery and continue into Metz on the D7. Metz was captured by the 10 and 11/KRRC in April 1917 and, despite the efforts of the German counterattack on 30 November, remained behind British lines until March 1918. It was retaken by the 1/Otago Regiment on 6 September 1918. After the war Metz was adopted by the County Borough of Halifax.

From Metz head northeast and take the D17 to Trescault, which was captured by the 20th Division on 21 April 1917, and remained in British hands until March 1918. It was finally recaptured by the 37th Division in September 1918. As you enter the village of Trescault you will come to a crossroads with a calvary mounted above the road on the right and a signpost pointing the way to Ribécourt and Marcoing. Continue straight on to the four-way intersection with the Mairie on the left and take the road to the left of the village war

Trescault Communal Cemetery.

memorial – **Rue de l'Égalité** – the Communal Cemetery is about 200m further along on the left.

Trescault Communal Cemetery contains seven casualties, six can be found on the left of the entrance and one in the rear right-hand corner. The only casualty of the Cambrai offensive is 21-year-old **Lieutenant Nathanial Pearce** (Headstone No. 6) of the 4/GG who died on 25 November. Appointed Battalion Transport Officer, he probably died of wounds received in Bourlon Wood after the battalion was sent to relieve the 2/Scots Guards. Where you are standing in the cemetery was the extreme left flank of the 153 Brigade attack towards Flesquières Ridge.

Retrace your steps to the intersection and turn sharp left along the D17 for approximately 600m to the battle-scarred **42nd (East Lancashire) Division Memorial** situated on the left of the road. The memorial was erected in recognition of the 42nd Division assault and capture of the Hindenburg Line in September 1918. But beware, it is easy to miss if you are driving. The 42nd Division did in fact apply to place their memorial in **Ribécourt Road Cemetery**, then called **Bilhem Farm Cemetery**, but were turned down by the IWGC, as it then was. The land that the memorial stands on was donated by Madame Bridour, on the condition that if the memorial ceased to exist in the future the land should revert to her heirs. The memorial was completed by 1921 and officially unveiled by Major General Solly-Flood on Easter Sunday in 1922.

To the left of the memorial is **Bilhem Farm**, where the cavalry had its headquarters on the morning of 20 November. In April 1917 Bilhem Farm was the last stronghold in the village to be captured by the 12/KRRC.

Continue for 200m to **Ribécourt Road Cemetery**, which you will see on the right. Before you enter glance across to the right towards **Beauchamps** which is where the H Battalion tanks were lined up along the ridge to the north of Beauchamp village in the dark waiting for zero hour. The village was taken by the 40th Division in April 1917.

The 42nd (East Lancashire) Division Memorial at Trescault.

Ribécourt Road Cemetery.

On entering the cemetery be aware that the 26 men who were killed in the Cambrai offensive are mainly buried in Plot 1, Rows B, C and D and these are largely men of 152 and 153 Brigade, 51st Division. The remaining plots were made in 1918 and are almost entirely composed of men of the 42nd Division. There are now 261 casualties and of these 9 are unidentified. There are three men of the Tank Corps here, probably the most well known of which is 23-year-old **Second Lieutenant William Haining** (I.B.1) of E Battalion, killed on 20 November. Haining was commissioned into the Machine Gun Corps in September 1916 and was the officer commanding E.27 *Ella*, named after his sister Isabella. Also killed on 20 November was one of the gunners in E.27, 19-year-old **Private Leslie Wray** (I.B.8), their tank was knocked out in the fields to the right of the D17 about 800m from the cemetery. The third man is 38-year-old **Private Albert Holman** (1.B.11) of D Battalion. If you are looking for a headstone on which to leave your cross of remembrance look no further than 34-year-old **Private William Newsome** (I.B.13) of the 2/6 West Yorks, who was killed on 20 November, probably in Havrincourt serving with 185 Brigade. Of the men of the 42nd Division the most decorated is 33-year-old **Private George Heard** (IV.B.1) of the 1/7 Lancashire Fusiliers, who received the MM and DCM before he was killed on 27 September 1918 along with 200 other men of the 42nd Division who were killed on the same day.

Leave the cemetery, turn right and drive down to the pumping station and stop. In the fields to the right was the approximate position of E.27 *Ella* and a little further along was the German front line of 20 November. Take a moment to imagine at least five tanks stuck in the wide trenches of the Hindenburg Line and abandoned on the left of the road and the whole landscape filled with advancing men. On the right was 152 Brigade pushing through the wire and further over was 71 Brigade heading for **Ribécourt**. A mile to the left is **Triangle Wood** and **Grand Ravine British Cemetery**, sitting on the eastern edge of Havrincourt.

Retrace your steps to the calvary and turn right on the D15 to Metz, following the road through Havrincourt Wood to Havrincourt, passing the track on the left leading to the former **Dean Copse** and the site of **Etna**, a German strongpoint. Continue along the D15, past the site of **Boggat Hole** on the right and, further on, the site of **Snowden**, both German strongpoints. The next junction is to the left, signposted **Hermies**, turn left here along the D5 for 550m and stop. The junction on the left leads down to the site of **Etna** and the whole of the junction where you are parked was dominated by **Vesuvius**, another German strongpoint (see **Route 1**). From the junction it is 600m to the Canal du Nord, and if you look to the north, you should get a good view of the **Spoilbank** on the left, which was taken by 109 Brigade (36th Division) on 20 November.

Retrace your steps to the junction with the D15 and after turning left continue into the centre of the village, pausing to look at the rather grand chateau on the right as you negotiate the roundabout. Continue to the village green on the right with the prominent village war memorial. It was here that **Second Lieutenant William McElroy** remained in his tank, G.3 *Gladiator*, for almost an hour keeping the enemy at bay after his tank was knocked out. The monument to the 62nd Division is 300m from here along Rue de Ribécourt.

Drive another 140m and turn right along a minor road, following the CWGC signpost for **Grand Ravine British Cemetery** (see **Route 1**). You may wish to walk the last 100m or so.

Retrace your steps and take the D15E2/D92 to **Flesquières**, which is opposite the village green and war memorial, passing the communal cemetery and **Chapel Wood** on the right. The road will take you to **Flesquières Communal Cemetery** where the D Battalion tank disaster occurred (see **Route 2**). From the cemetery continue straight on across the village, avoiding the right turn as it is one-way

Grand Ravine British Cemetery.

only. At the church you should be able to rejoin the D92 along Rue de l'Église, noting the former site of the watering hole on the left. **Flesquières Hill British Cemetery** is on the D89 on the outskirts of the village next to the Cambrai Tank Museum. Those of you wishing to spend more time in Flesquières should consult **Route 2**.

Retrace your steps to the crossroads – signposted D89 Ribécourt and Gouzeaucourt – and turn left, stopping by the **Monument of Nations** on the left. The site of the E Battalion disaster was in the fields to your left (if you are facing Ribécourt). From the memorial drive downhill to **Ribécourt**, passing over the former railway line and embankment (see **Route 2**). To the right at the crossroads is the Mairie and at the end of the road is the site of the Victoria Cross action of **Lance Corporal McBeath**, whilst straight on is the church and bridge over the **Grand Ravine**. The tour concludes here.

Appendix I
VC Winners during the Cambrai Offensive

Nineteen Victoria Crosses were awarded during the seventeen days of the Cambrai offensive, seven of which were posthumous. Five of these men have no known grave and are commemorated on the Cambrai Memorial at Louveral and two rest in communal cemeteries.

Name	Date of Action	Where	Reference
McBeath, L/Cpl Robert *1/5 Seaforth Highlanders*	20 November	Ribécourt	Murdered whilst a policeman in Vancouver in 1922
Shepherd, Rifleman Albert *12 KRRC*	20 November	Villers-Plouich	Died Royston in 1966
Sherwood-Kelly, Lt/Col John *1 Royal Inniskilling Fusiliers*	20 November	Marcoing	Died London in 1931
Spackman, Sgt Charles *1 Borders*	20 November	Marcoing	Died Southampton in 1969
Strachan, Lt Harcus *Fort Garry Horse*	20 November	Masnières	Died Vancouver in 1982
Wain, Capt Richard *A Battalion, Tank Corps*	20 November	Marcoing	Cambrai Memorial
McAulay, Sgt John *1 Scots Guards*	27 November	Fortaine-Notre-Dame	Died Glasgow in 1956

Name	Date of Action	Where	Reference
Clare, Private George *5 Lancers*	28/29 November	Bourlon Wood	Cambrai Memorial
Elliott-Cooper, Lt/Col Neville *8 Royal Fusiliers*	30 November	La Vacquerie	Died Hannover in 1918 whilst a POW
Gee, Capt Robert *2 Royal Fusiliers*	30 November	Masnières	Died Perth in 1960
Gourley, Sgt Cyril *D Battery, CCXLVI Brigade RFA*	30 November	Epehy	Died Haslemere in 1982
Stone, Capt Walter *17 Royal Fusiliers*	30 November	Rat's Tail Trench	Cambrai Memorial
Thomas, L/Cpl John *2/5 North Staffords*	30 November	Fontaine-Notre-Dame	Died Stockport in 1954
Wallace, Lt Samuel *C Battery, LXIII Brigade RFA*	30 November	Gonnelieu	Died in Edinburgh in 1968
McReady-Diarmid, Capt Allastair *17 Middlesex*	30 November	Mœuvres	Cambrai Memorial
Singh, Lance-Dafadar Gobind *2 Lancers*	1 December	Peizière	Died Nagaur, India, in 1942
Paton, Capt George *4 Grenadier Guards*	1 December	Gonnelieu	Metz-en-Couture Communal Cemetery Extension (II.E.24)

Name	Date of Action	Where	Reference
Lascelles, Capt Arthur *14 DLI*	3 December	Marcoing	Killed 1918 and buried at Dourlers Communal Cemetery Extension (II.G.24)
Emerson, 2/Lt James *9 Royal Inniskilling Fusiliers*	6 December	La Vacquerie	Cambrai Memorial

Appendix 2

Writers, Artists, Poets and Composers who Took Part in the Cambrai Offensive

The only officer killed outside the official dates of the Cambrai offensive was Lieutenant Commander Robert Shaw-Stewart RNVR, commanding the Hood Battalion, who was killed on Welsh Ridge during a German counterattack. He has been included because the fighting on Welsh Ridge continued well past 7 December. Perhaps the most well known of the men listed below are Henry Moore and John Nash, but the poetry of Ewart Mackintosh is well worth reading particularly as his verse was once described as being as good as the more famous war poet Rupert Brooke. Mackintosh's poem 'In Memoriam', dedicated to Private David Sutherland, is particularly masterful.

Date of Death	Name	Designation	Reference
21 Nov. 1917	**Mackintosh**, Lieutenant Ewart *1/5 Seaforth Highlanders*	Poet	A Highland Regiment and Other Poems War, the Liberator and Other Pieces Ghosts of War
1949	**Lee**, 2/Lieutenant Joseph *10 KRRC*	Poet, writer and artist	Ballads of Battle and Work-a-Day Warriors. *A Captive in Carlsruhe & Other German Prison Camps* (book)
26 Sep. 1947	**Lofting**, 2/Lieutenant Hugh *1 Irish Guards*	Novelist and poet	The Doctor Doolittle books

Appendix 2 • 173

Date of Death	Name	Designation	Reference
27 Mar. 1975	**Bliss,** 2/Lieutenant Arthur 1 Grenadier Guards	Composer	Morning Heroes The Olympians A Colour Symphony
31 Aug. 1986	**Moore,** Private Henry *15 London Regiment*	Sculptor	Family Group Draped Reclining Woman Oval With Points
30 Dec. 1917	**Shaw-Stewart** Lt/Com Patrick *Hood Battalion RNVR*	Poet	I Saw a Man this Morning Achilles in the Trench
17 Feb. 1985	**Coppard,** Cpl George *37 Company, Machine Gun Corps*	Writer	*With a Machine Gun to Cambrai* (book)
?	**Blicq,** Private Stanley *1 Royal Guernsey Light Infantry*	Writer and poet	*Norman Ten Hundred* (book)
Sep. 1977	**Nash,** Sergeant John (brother of Paul Nash) *28 London Regiment (Artists Rifles)*	War artist	Over the Top Oppy Wood 1917, Evening
Aug. 1969	**Marsden,** 2/Lieutenant Walter *2/4 Loyal North Lancs*	Sculptor and poet	St Anne's on Sea War Memorial Bolton War Memorial Heywood War Memorial
1969	**Thomas,** A/Captain Alan *6 Royal West Kents*	Writer	*A Life Apart* (book) *The Director Daggers Drawn*
1969	**Rowberry,** Sergeant Claude *D Battalion Tank Corps*	Artist	Menin Road Fighting Birds Götterdämmerung, Albert

FURTHER READING

Four of the **Battleground Europe** titles published by Pen & Sword – www.pen-and-sword.co.uk – focus on the area covered in this guidebook and provide a host of supplementary information. In these books you will find contemporary photographs of soldiers and venues in the Cambrai offensive, as well as battlefield maps and personal accounts:

Mitchinson, Bill, *Villers-Plouich and the Five Ridges*, 2001
Horsfall, Jack and Nigel Cave, *Cambrai the Right Hook*, 1999
Horsfall, Jack and Nigel Cave, *Flesquières, Bourlon Wood*, 2002

Apart from regimental and divisional histories, the battle has generated a wealth of literature of its own, some of which has been used in this guidebook. Of these, the following may be of interest:

Gibot, Jean-Luc and Philippe Gorczynski, *Following the Tanks*, privately published
Hickey, Daniel, *Rolling Into Action*, Naval & Military Press, 2007
Watson, W.H.L., *A Company of Tanks*, Echo Library, 2014
Blicq, Stanley, *Norman Ten Hundred*, Echo Library, 2009
Carrington, Charles, *Soldier from the Wars Returning*, Hutchinson, 1965
Browne, Douglas, *The Tank in Action*, BibloLife, 2009
Coppard, George, *With a Machine Gun to Cambrai*, Macmillan, 1986
Moore, William, *A Wood Called Bourlon*, Leo Cooper, 1988
Taylor, John, *Deborah and the War of the Tanks*, Pen & Sword, 2016
Sheldon, Jack, *The German Army at Cambrai*, Pen & Sword 2009
Thomas, Alan, *A Life Apart*, Gollancz, 1968
Gliddon, Gerald, *VCs Handbook, The Western Front 1914–1918*, Sutton, 2005

There are several other guides that refer to Cambrai; Major and Mrs Holt's *Guide to the Western Front South* devotes a section to the area whilst the late Rose Combes refers to Cambrai in *Before Endeavours Fade*. Another useful section on Cambrai is to be found in *A New*

Guide to the Battlefields of Northern France by Michael Glover. For battlefield visitors who wish to expand their knowledge in more depth the more recent *Cambrai 1917, The Myth of the First Great Tank Battle* by Bryn Hammond (Phoenix, 2009) is worthy of further study as is the earlier *Ironclads of Cambrai* by Bryan Cooper (Pan Books, 1967). The Osprey book by Alexander Turner, *Cambrai 1917, The Birth of Armoured Warfare*, is also recommended. The story of the Tank Corps is well told by Frank Mitchell in *Tank Warfare, The Story of Tanks in the Great War*, another book by Captain J.R.W. Murland recounts the development of the Tank Corps from its inception to the dark days of 1942 in *The Royal Armoured Corps*.

INDEX

Bleak House, 158, 159
Boggat Hole, 19, 22, 23, 167
Bonavis crossroads, 134
Bourlon, 1, 5, 11, 12, 14, 45, 50, 51, 54, 55, 60, 61–2, 63, 64, 66, 68, 69, 76–92, 148, 150, 164
Butler's Cross, 22

Canal de Saint-Quentin, 6
Canal du Nord, 6, 19, 22, 45, 47, 48, 147
cemeteries
    Anneux British Cem., 90, 91, 148
    Bilhem Farm Cem., 164
    Boursies Communal Cem., 49
    Bourlon Wood Cem., 90, 148
    Cambrai East German Cem., 3
    Cantaign British Cem., 2, 74, 150
    Crest Cem. 68
    Demicourt Communal Cem., 46, 47, 147
    Fifteen Ravine British Cem., 127–8, 158, 159, 160
    Flesquières British Cem., 36, 168
    Fontaine Communal Cem., 70–1, 167
    Gonnelieu Communal Cem., 129, 139
    Gouzeaucourt New Britsh Cem., 129, 144, 161
    Graincourt Communal Cem., 55–60, 59
    Grand Ravine British Cem., 19, 25, 31, 32 166, 167
    Hermies Hill British Cem., 47
    Louveral Military Cem., 53–4, 146
    Lowrie Cem., 25
    Marcoing British Cem., 93, 104, 105, 156
    Marcoing Communal Cem., 102, 103, 156
    Masnières British Cem., 2, 117
    Metz-en-Couture Communal Cem., 162–3
    Mœuvres British Cem., 49, 147
    Mœuvres Communal Cem. Extension, 49, 50, 147
    Noyelles-sur-Escaut Communal Cem., 155
    Orival Wood Cem., 67, 152–5
    Ribécourt British Cem., 43
    Ribécourt Railway Cem. 31
    Ribécourt Road Cem., 164–6
    Rue de la Haut Communal Cem., 39
    Ruyaulcourt Military Cem., 73, 151
    Trescault Communal Cem., 164
    Villers-Plouich Communal Cem., 120, 121
Corner Work, 118, 123, 125, 159
Crèvecoeur, 38, 107, 108, 109, 110, 117

Dean Copse, 19, 23, 166

equivalent ranks, 3
Etna, 19, 22, 23, 166

Fermy Wood, 22, 26
Flesquières, 28–44, 30–1, 32, 33, 34–5, 36, 37, 42–3, 48, 58, 61, 64, 67, 120, 153, 164, 167
Flot Farm, 102

Gauche Wood, 141, 142
Gin Trench, 138, 160
Gouzeaucourt, 58, 129
Gouzeaucourt and Gonnelieu, 130–45
Gouzeaucourt Wood, 9, 132, 161, 162
Grand Ravine, 19, 25, 26, 31, 32, 166, 168

Halberstadt CL.II, 13, 14
Havrincourt, 6, 7, 8, 9, 11, 19–27, 30, 31, 62, 120, 134, 166

Index • 177

Havrincourt Chateau, 19
Havrincourt Wood, 7, 9, 19, 20, 134, 166
Hindenburg Line, 6, 6, 7, 11, 19, 45, 48, 49, 52, 93, 118, 119, 122, 125, 159, 156, 166
historical context, 4–14
Hotel Beatus, 15
Hubert Road (Havrincourt Wood), 7, 21, 22

Lateau Wood, 128, 157, 158
Le Quennet Farm, 157
Les Baraques, 159

Mark IV tank, 7, 8, 9, 10, 39
Masnières and Marcoing, 97–117
memorials
    42 (East Lancashire) Mem., 164, 165
    62nd Division Mem., 25, 26
    Boursies War Mem., 47
    Cambrai Mem., 46, 52–3, 146
    Cambrai Tank Museum, 36, 37
    Canadian Mem. (Bourlon), 90, 91, 148, 149
    Ewart Mackintosh Mem., 65, 66
    Fort Garry Horse Mem., 110, 111
    Gouzeaucourt War Mem., 135
    Graham Lyall Mem. (Bourlon), 86, 148
    Graincourt War Mem., 58
    Havincourt War Mem., 26
    Hostetter Mem., 112
    Masnières War Mem., 111, 112
    Monument of Nations (Flesquières), 36, 37

Newfoundland Caribou Mem., 116, 117, 156
RGLI Mem., 115
Villers-Plouich War Mem., 120
Mœuvres, 6, 45–54, 82, 85, 88, 147

Noyelles, 9, 30, 64, 74, 93, 94, 98, 154, 155, 156

Oxford Valley, 21

Pan Pan Farm, 157
Plough Support Trench, 28

Queen's Cross, 132, 151, 162
Quentin Mill, 129, 141, 142, 143, 144

Royal Flying Corps (RFC), 13
Rumilly, 97, 102, 105, 106

Shropshire Spur, 22
Snowden, 19, 23, 169
Spoilbank, 45, 48, 167
summary of routes, 18

Talma Chateau, 101, 102
Trescault, 9, 20, 21, 22, 23, 30, 43, 163, 164
Triangle Wood, 22

Vesuvius, 19, 22, 166
Village Road, 118, 122, 123, 126, 127
Villers-Plouich and La Vacquerie, 118–28

Welsh Ridge, 159, 163, 172
Welsh Road, 118, 122, 123, 124
Winter Line, 13